D0371794

Praise for

conscious loving
EVER AFTER

"In *Conscious Loving Ever After,* Katie and Gay Hendricks don't
just give relationship advice, they radiate wisdom and joy on every
page. This book will transform and enrich the way you and your partner
experience each other—and yourselves. I hope you will read it, come
to see love in a new light, and relish the opportunity to
spend time with these incredible souls."

— **Iyanla Vanzant,** *New York Times* best-selling author of
In the Meantime and *One Day My Soul Just Opened Up*

"If you ask me, Katie and Gay are the perfect exemplars of conscious,
loving, ever evolving, and utterly fabulous relationships. When I grow
up I want to be just like them. This wise, generous book shows you how
to do what they've done and live with passion, clarity, and joy."

— **Geneen Roth,** author of *Women, Food and God*

"Kathlyn and Gay Hendricks have mastered the art of Conscious
Loving and generously share their decades of wisdom in this original
and powerful book that provides life-transforming tools for your
love life. Whether you've been married for years or are ready to
re-enter the dating world, this book offers a clear path to
creating the relationship of your dreams."

— **Arielle Ford,** author of *The Soulmate Secret*

"*Conscious Loving Ever After* provides couples and singles in
the second half of life a joyful and creative map for the journey.
If you want to make the most of your loving relationships at
midlife and beyond, read this book!"

— **Jack Canfield,** co-author, *Chicken Soup for the Soul*®
and *The Success Principles*™

conscious loving
EVER AFTER

Also by Gay Hendricks and Kathlyn Hendricks

Spirit-Centered Relationships *
Attracting Genuine Love
Lasting Love
Breathing Ecstasy
The Conscious Heart
At the Speed of Life
Radiance
Conscious Loving
Centering and the Art of Intimacy
The Moving Center

Also by Gay Hendricks

The Tenzing Norbu Mystery Series (with Tinker Lindsay)*
The Big Leap
Five Wishes (with Neale Donald Walsch)
You've Got to Read This Book (with Jack Canfield)
Conscious Golf
Bodymind Vibrance
Conscious Living
The Centered Athlete (with Jon Carlson)
Learning to Love Yourself
Transpersonal Approaches to Counseling and Psychotherapy (with Barry Weinhold)
The Centered Teacher
The Family Centering Book
How to Love Every Minute of Your Life (with Carol Leavenworth)
The Second Centering Book (with Thomas B. Roberts)
Transpersonal Education (ed., with James Fadiman)
The Centering Book (with Russell Wills)

*Available from Hay House

Please visit:

Hay House USA: www.hayhouse.com®
Hay House Australia: www.hayhouse.com.au
Hay House UK: www.hayhouse.co.uk
Hay House South Africa: www.hayhouse.co.za
Hay House India: www.hayhouse.co.in

conscious loving
EVER AFTER

HOW TO CREATE THRIVING
RELATIONSHIPS
AT MIDLIFE AND BEYOND

Gay Hendricks, Ph.D., &
Kathlyn Hendricks, Ph.D.

HAY HOUSE, INC.
Carlsbad, California • New York City
London • Sydney • Johannesburg
Vancouver • Hong Kong • New Delhi

Published and distributed in the United States by: Hay House, Inc.: www.hayhouse.com® • *Published and distributed in Australia by:* Hay House Australia Pty. Ltd.: www.hayhouse.com.au • *Published and distributed in the United Kingdom by:* Hay House UK, Ltd.: www.hayhouse .co.uk • *Published and distributed in the Republic of South Africa by:* Hay House SA (Pty), Ltd.: www.hayhouse.co.za • *Distributed in Canada by:* Raincoast Books: www.raincoast.com • *Published in India by:* Hay House Publishers India: www.hayhouse.co.in

Cover design: Angela Moody • *Interior design:* Pam Homan
Illustrations: Donna Arrogante, www.donnaarrogante.com

Library of Congress Cataloging-in-Publication Data

Hendricks, Gay.
 Conscious loving ever after : how to create thriving relationships at midlife and beyond / Gay Hendricks and Kathlyn Hendricks. -- 1st edition.
    pages cm
   ISBN 978-1-4019-4732-3 (hardback)
 1. Man-woman relationships. 2. Intimacy (Psychology) 3. Middle-aged persons. 4. Older people. 5. Sex. I. Hendricks, Kathlyn. II. Title.
  HQ801.H4557 2015
  306.7--dc23
                                        2015010381

Hardcover ISBN: 978-1-4019-4732-3

10 9 8 7 6 5 4 3 2 1
1st edition, October 2015

Printed in the United States of America

*To our community of friends,
students, and colleagues—now three
generations strong—thank you for
joining us in co-creating a new
world of relationships
on our beloved planet.*

CONTENTS

Introduction: Discovering the Fountain of Youth in Love   xi

Chapter One: Creativity Calling   1

Chapter Two: Integrity Is Sexy   27

Chapter Three: Full-Spectrum Presencing   55

Chapter Four: The Best Sex Ever   77

Chapter Five: Blame-Free Relationships   95

Chapter Six: From Fear to Flow with the Four Fear-Melters   111

Chapter Seven: Facing Death and Loss in Relationships   129

Chapter Eight: Two Ten-Minute Conversations a Week   145

Chapter Nine: How to Attract a Conscious Loving Relationship   161

Chapter Ten: Conscious Loving Online   173

Afterword   189

Appendix A: Six Whole-Body Learning Activities for Couples,
     Singles, and Professionals   191

   1. *The Rule of Three Process:*
       Getting New Insight into Your Relationships   193

   2. *The Love Catalyst for Couples:*
       A Deep Experience of Full-Spectrum Presencing   199

   3. *The Love Catalyst for Singles:*
       Full-Spectrum Presencing to Attract the Love of Your Life   203

   4. *The Genius of Relationship Process:*
       Liberating Your Hidden Creativity   208

   5. *Unhooking the Source:*
       That Was Then, This Is Now   212

   6. *Customizing Your Appreciation:*
       The Most Reliable Way to Renew Intimacy   215

Appendix B: The Four Pillars of Integrity   217

Further Resources   221

Acknowledgments   222

About the Authors   223

Introduction

Discovering the Fountain of Youth in Love

Are you passionately dedicated to experiencing your full capacity for love during your time here on earth?

If so, you are in for a thrilling ride on the greatest journey imaginable—and you're embarking at the perfect time. We've discovered that the time from midlife onward offers the greatest opportunity of any life stage to grow in love. We'll say it even plainer: *you can have more beautiful love and more passionate sex in the years from midlife onward than you ever had before.*

We met for the first time in 1980, as colleagues who had admired each other's work from a distance, when Gay came to teach a weekend seminar at the graduate school where Katie taught. About ten seconds later, though, we had a profound mind/ heart meld that has lasted to this day. We started living and work-ing together within months of meeting each other, and as we've often told couples seeking our counsel about working together, working with your mate is like being in perpetual training for the Relationship Olympics. There's no time off!

We happen to love the exhilaration of being in the Olym-pics all the time. The air definitely breathes a little sweeter there, although you have to do some training to cultivate a body that can handle that much good feeling. You'll find out how to do all that as we go along in the book.

Our special focus for the last 20 years has been to help people enjoy lasting love in the years from midlife onward. We met in our early 30s, so by the time we entered the phase called "midlife" in our 40s, we had already faced and survived a number of challenges to our relationship. These challenges included being broke and in debt, struggling with health issues, taking care of aging parents, raising two kids, remodeling a hundred-year-old house, and other stresses we've mercifully forgotten. However, even if you rolled all of those challenges up into a large bundle, it was nothing compared to what we were about to experience.

If you want to find out if your marriage is as solid as you think it is, write a best-selling relationship book and go on Oprah a couple of times. After Oprah featured *Conscious Loving* on her show in the early '90s, we went suddenly from the quiet life of a university professor and a private-practice therapist to getting stopped in airports for autographs and snapshots. We had poured all we'd learned about the power of authenticity, healthy responsibility, and commitment into *Conscious Loving*. People responded to our story and the many examples of *how* to create conscious loving throughout the book. We had also introduced a revolutionary concept that has become a cornerstone of our work: the Upper Limit Problem, which you'll read more about later in this book as well. The ceiling that people unconsciously place on their ability to give and receive love basically means we get challenged by things going well—and this was exactly what we were about to discover. The sudden influx of attention and money took a toll on our relationship; it brought shadow parts of us we'd never known about to the surface and gave us a chance to expand our own upper limits.

For example, Gay's eye wandered for the first time in 15 years, to settle upon a 25-year-old with whom he had a brief (and thankfully nonsexual) flirtation. Even though it's something we laugh about now, we definitely didn't do much laughing about it at the time. It took us months and many of the Ten-Minute Talks you'll learn about later in the book to get through that challenge and many others we faced.

Our own relationship is our first and most important living laboratory. This is important for us to mention because long before we ever teach a relationship concept or tool in our seminars, we've tested it out thoroughly on ourselves. One of the signature features of our work is that everything we teach is not only kitchen tested, but also bedroom and boardroom tested in our own relationship and the businesses we run.

We believe our own marriage has survived and thrived because we've used the ideas and tools you'll discover in the pages ahead. There's no way to know for sure if we would have ultimately split up or stayed together, but at midlife we were at a low point in our marriage when we made the life-changing decision to rebirth our own relationship.

We'd been married about 15 years by the time the post-Oprah shadows emerged, and had fallen into comfortable roles and routines that resulted in a kind of staleness and loss of intimacy between us. We'd both put on weight, but the real source of our malaise was not our plump bodies—it was that we had drifted away from our essential connection. We were traveling constantly, eating rich restaurant food, and laser focused on filling the auditorium for the next seminar. A few years of this adrenaline-based lifestyle took its toll. Our bank account was growing abundantly along with our waist sizes, but our inner reserves were drawn down to the point where we looked at each other one day and said, "What are we doing this for?" We had lost the special feeling between us that had made us so passionate about teaching our work in the first place. Gay's flirtation gave us a chance to test all the practices we wrote about in *Conscious Loving*. We kept returning to what was most deeply true and speaking as authentically as we knew how. Sharing raw feelings and bringing old fears and judgments to the surface polished away our learned masks and opened new lenses to love. Sitting on the debris heap of the old patterns, we looked at each other and realized that we still recognized the crackling essence sparks that had drawn us together in the first place. We got messy, and then we recommitted to each other and to love.

Since then, our explorations in our own life and in our seminars and client work have taken us on an even deeper dive. Rather than simply helping people work through traditional issues—power struggles, communication breakdowns, money, and sex—we've tapped into a new source of energy and rejuvenation for relationships in the second half of life.

We've put the best of those tools—the ones that generate more love, creativity, and passion in the lives of people at midlife and beyond—in this book. Through the daily practice of those tools, we found our way through crisis after crisis to discover, ultimately, the fountain of youth in love.

The Fountain of Youth in Love

In a moment we'll jump into Chapter One, where we will show you the most remarkable discovery we've made so far, the most powerful tool you'll need for bringing more love into your life from your midlife years on. It's a discovery that still amazes us to this day: that our human quest to feel the full amount of love we can give and receive is also a quest to discover the creative wellspring deep within us all.

As you'll discover throughout the book, creativity flows from a central choice we all make in the second half of life. Are you going to expand beyond your current patterns and pictures of relating or fold up into routines and fixed beliefs? Are you going to re-create yourself again and again or settle and compromise? Many people choose to sink into familiar roles, old stories, and viewpoints, and their contracting bodies and rote loving reflect it. We want to show you how creating and playing can replace surviving with thriving. We know that it's never too late to experience the juiciness of genuine presence and the flow of renewal inside you and in love.

We believe there actually is a new fountain of love you can tap into at midlife and later. However, we still marvel, as you probably will, at the paradoxical path we all must take to get there. We can only get to ultimate intimacy with another person by being willing to embark on a journey we can take only on our own.

When you make a deep commitment to your own creative magnificence—to expressing the unique organic genius that lives in potential within us all—your relationships get better as a result. In other words, your deep commitment to your own creative liberation creates good feeling and harmony in your relationships. All it takes is one person in a relationship to get the magic started. But when two people in a relationship open up to their full creative expression, miracles happen fast and often. Miracles such as:

- The rebirth of sexual passion in a marriage after a seven-year drought

- A 54-year-old who had given up on love suddenly making an inner shift and drawing an entirely new kind of person into her life

- The marriage of a 59-year-old woman who had vowed when she was 20 never to get married until women could marry women

- Two widowers shedding the painful past and feeling the blossoming of new love in their 60s

The Fine Print

Now, take a deep breath with us and embrace a fact of relationship transformation at midlife and beyond: it isn't always easy and it isn't always pleasant. Strange as it may sound, though, we have found that it's always as hard and as unpleasant as it needs to be. Something has to get our attention, to snap us out of the trance of old programming and wake us up to the flow of love in the present.

As you have probably noticed, we humans often need to create major dramas in our lives to wake ourselves up. For example, some people may read a book on healthy eating, get the message, implement the changes the book suggests, and effortlessly lose 40 pounds. We don't know any of those people. However, we have intimate knowledge of two people, both of whom had 40 pounds to lose, who had several dozen diet and health books on their shelves but didn't stop eating foods that were harming them until after their habits sent them into a health crisis. We know those people quite well because they are us! Now, 40 pounds lighter, we're glad we got the message, even though it took a virtual whack on the head to get our attention.

In the same way, people in troubled relationships often don't change direction until they crash into a wall of some kind. Of course, it would be more pleasant if we all awakened ourselves gracefully, as in "Oh dear, I seem to have been taking my spouse for granted for the past few years. I think I'll make some radical changes starting today!" However, most of us don't awaken from relationship trances with such good-natured aplomb and willingness to take on the task.

Count yourself among the blessed, because you have already had moments of awakening. We hope yours weren't as unpleasant as some of our own moments you'll read about. We suspect, though, you have had your moments of intense pain either in your singlehood or in the intimacies of your love relationships. That's what got you here, and our congratulations to you for finding your way through it to a place of curiosity and openness to growth.

Now the real journey can begin. Once we awaken ourselves from the unfulfilling trances of the past, we face the heroic task of disentangling ourselves from the various levels of *unconscious* loving that most of us truss ourselves up in by midlife. Fortunately, there are only a handful of mistakes that block the flow of love. The problem is that we tend to keep making those mistakes relentlessly, even zealously, over and over again. The good news is that the book you're holding is full of breakthrough solutions. We encourage you to dedicate a little regular time to learning how to use the tools we'll offer throughout the book and in detail in the Appendices. If you do, you'll possess a set of lifetime skills that will reliably get you through the stuck places and open the flow of love, even if the flow has been dried up for years.

Enmeshed, Entangled, and Encumbered

Some couples finish each other's sentences. Some people can't make a decision without consultation and handholding. And some people feel burdened by another's unwillingness to change or grow. These are some of the top complaints of both singles and partners later in life. The varieties of unconscious loving that people seem to get away with in youth start to crystallize at midlife and beyond.

That crystallization starts corroding your energy level, your physical health, and every aspect of your life. When people favor getting and doing rather than being, crystallizing disconnects them from the direct experience of love and can rigidify into unconscious loving. When singles or partners get very busy providing, building careers, and handling the business of life, they can lose touch with the intimacy and possibilities for joy that the business is supposed to support. The very breath of connection gets smothered by lists and deadlines. Love, no longer prioritized, becomes routine.

Unconscious loving seeps in through a very simple but profoundly impactful choice: people simply stop giving themselves and others loving attention. We now know that humans need attention as much as they need food and water. The loving touch, the genuine appreciation that created intimacy on the first few dates or in the first years of union easily fade into "Love ya, babe" flybys.

The biggest mistake, though, is to tamp down your creative juice, choice by choice, until your days and your relating feel flat and repetitive. Spontaneity turns to routine, and playful passion to painful distance. Here's the problem with dampening down your creativity over time: in the absence of creative variety, people tend to create drama, because drama provides the jolt of adrenaline to replace the thrill that's gone. Routine activities, escalating conflict, and power struggles replace the deep intimacy of open contact and become the norm. Here's a great example: when we told an interviewer we hadn't had a conflict for many years, there was a long pause, and then she said, "Well, what do you talk about?!"

Despite your past choices and mistakes, the real future of your relationships doesn't have to keep devolving. Your future is right here, right now, in the choices you make about whether or not to expand in love in a conscious way.

The Future Is Now

Years ago we visualized a new world of relationships. In this bright new future, all of us would speak to each other honestly from the first date instead of withholding important feelings and facts from each other. In the new world we would all take responsibility for meeting challenges instead of looking for people to blame or shouldering love as a burden. In the future we'd all know how to tap into our unique creative genius, we'd live in relationships that nurtured that genius, and we'd beam a steady flow of appreciation to each other as we went about the daily task of bringing forth our genius.

That's the future world we visualized, and since we didn't see it happening in the world we actually lived in, we realized we were going to have to start the revolution at home. So we did. We decided we were going to do everything we could to show up reliably in our relationship as honest, responsible, grateful, and in touch with our creative genius. Those were big, powerful intentions, and when we made them, we had no idea it would take us years of conscious attention to get through all the murky barriers of our old programming.

However, every bit of that work was worth "a price above rubies," as one of our grandmothers would say. For example, it took us several years of conscious attention to eliminate criticism and blame from our relationship. The payoff from the effort, though, has been massive and radical: it's been well over a decade since either of us has uttered a critical word to the other. In fact, we haven't had an argument yet this century! Many people find that kind of relationship hard to conceptualize. That's why we call it a radical change. It still seems astonishing to us, even though we know how much dedicated attention it took to create the magic of a blame-free relationship. We know what it feels like to go from years of bickering to years of an unbroken flow of appreciation, co-creativity, and openhearted communication. It's genuinely awesome; we feel awe about it every day.

You can make that kind of magic for yourself. The magic comes from moments of choice, in which you choose to expand in love rather than contract in fear. In those moments you create a new destiny in love. This is such a moment for you—a moment to choose your new destiny—and this is a book of action steps and tools that can take you there. We want you to use this book as a practical manual for increasing the felt experience of love and creativity in your life. We'll be showing you the key concepts and central practices that can take you from routine to renewal and from impasse to passion. You'll hear stories of transformation from singles and couples in heterosexual and same-sex partnerships putting these processes in play in their lives. You'll learn powerful ways to produce magic in your relationships throughout later life. We want you to bring the future of love into your life, right now. We've seen that future and it's already here. Now let's make it happen for *you*.

CHAPTER ONE

Creativity Calling

We have a gift for you. It's a gift we first gave ourselves many years ago, a blessing we gave ourselves that keeps on nurturing our own relationship to this day. The gift is a deep connection with your own creative essence—the sacred spark deep within yourself that keeps you looking for ways to love more and feel more engaged with your creative passions.

What does your creative essence have to do with your relationships?

Everything!

Here's why:

Your creative essence is who you really are, the unique spark of aliveness that makes you the one-of-a-kind person you are. It's the singular, precious part of you without which, if it were taken away, you wouldn't be *you*. In our work together in this book, you will have the opportunity to open yourself fully to your own creative essence and use its amazing flow to rebirth a rich new experience of love in your life.

Speaking personally, we lost touch with that magical creative part of ourselves somewhere in the growing-up process. By the time we were in our 20s we were so out of contact with our creative essence that we didn't even know it existed. Fortunately, through a combination of good luck and dedicated attention, we were able to reconnect with that precious part of ourselves and make it the foundation of our relationship. Working with thousands of people since then has only strengthened our conviction that a new relationship with your own creative essence is the secret to lasting love in the years from midlife onward.

Our own experience over the last four decades has given us a deep respect for the power of creative regeneration to restore relationships, to enliven life in general, and even to contribute to the healing of physical ailments. When people get into deeper communication with their own individual creative essence, their relationships blossom as a direct result. As you use the tools in this book, you'll probably realize that by opening up a deeper conversation with your inner creative source, you're sending a new wave of energy through your whole life. In our own case, the choices we made at midlife and the tools we applied—the same tools you're learning in this book—took us to a level of health we never had dreamed possible. Not only have we both shed the 40 extra pounds of prosperity padding we had accumulated by the time we turned 50, we've also both been able to get off medications we'd been on, such as cholesterol-lowering and blood-pressure-lowering drugs.

Connecting with Your Creative Essence

Many people, when they hear the words *creativity* or *creative expression,* probably think of a specific tool such as journaling or a hobby such as macramé. Your creative essence is something much more fundamental than any specific hobby or tool. Your creative essence is the power to surprise yourself. If writing is one of your creative tools, as it is for us, your creative essence is in charge when you have those moments of "Aha!" as you're writing. Something new and intriguing comes forth that you didn't know was there.

You don't have to be a writer or an artist or any particular type of person to get your creative essence on the line—in fact, it's important to realize that creativity is available in everyone's life. In the next ten minutes you could summon forth your creative essence and put it to work for you in many different ways, all with no tools other than your natural gift of awareness.

For example, you could make yourself a creative snack, a new assemblage you've never tried before. Go to the kitchen and let yourself be drawn to a few interesting items, but this time put special attention on combining things into new configurations you've never eaten. For example, one of Gay's favorite snacks is an apple cut into very thin slices. Recently he's been adding creative touches to it, such as a dab of nut butter on a slice, topped by a thin slice of radish. Some of the experiments work, others don't the addition of capers was a particularly bad idea—but they all fit the criteria of being brand new and never before tasted.

What Kind of Creativity Do We Recommend?

Here's a practical definition of the kind of creativity that opens up new vistas in love: creativity is anything that opens awareness of new ways your body and mind can play. For example, in addition to journaling, playing music, and doing movement practices every day, Katie also takes delight in cooking as a form of creative expression. Pretty much anything that can give your body and mind a stretch will work wonders in your love life. Living on a constant personal growth mission gives you a zest that increases your attraction quotient. The act of creating vibrates the tuning fork of your deepest aliveness and ripples those waves of delight through you and to others. Later in the book you'll see how your personal tuning fork vibration ripples even more fully within the structure that integrity provides.

If you're a couple, you owe it to yourselves to find out if creativity can create the kind of transformation we're describing in your relationship. Connecting with your creative essence is not hard or complicated. It just requires dedication. It seemed hard to us at first, but it turned out we were looking through the fog of our old programming: it was hard only because that programming was keeping us from seeing new possibilities. It's a miracle of existence

3

that the creative essence of human beings always rests there in the background, even if we haven't accessed it in years. Fortunately for all of us, it doesn't go anywhere; it sits there waiting for us to summon it. Once you have it flowing in your life, you have a new compass to guide you. Every decision you make can be evaluated with a simple question: *Will this path of action lead to a deeper connection with my creative essence or take me farther away from it?*

How Does Creativity Feel in Your Body?

As you deepen your connection with your creative essence, you also get to enjoy one of the most unusual positive feelings available to human beings. You actually feel a different way in your body, and the feeling is a unique one. It's a combination of ease, delight, and energetic flow. One of our clients described the feeling as "kind of like making love all the time on the inside of myself, even if I was walking down the street with my clothes on." She was obviously having a very good day, but even on an average day the sense of excitement and engagement that comes from being in harmony with your creative essence feels delicious in the body.

You can tune in to and enjoy the flow of creating more and more in your daily life. As you do, you'll probably notice that it's not *what* you create that gives you fulfillment, it's *that* you create consciously. Here's Katie describing her experience of creating:

> People often think that to be of value, creating must produce a thing or an event, a measurable project or item that can be consumed. And of course creativity results in innovations, new systems and ways of operating. That misses the big point about creativity, though, which is the joy of the experience itself. What I feel in my body keeps me recommitting to my creative process, the soul-satisfying flow of being in the slipstream of newness. My dance-movement therapy mentor, Mary Whitehouse, used to talk about the distinction between moving and "being moved." Creativity is being moved by your openness to what's emerging, being able to notice and catch the first stirrings of something coming into being.

I open the gateway to a full-body experience of creativity with curious attention. When I swirl my curious awareness through my body, I experience a whole-body "hmmm" dancing around inside. The interior of my body feels lighter. Rather than awareness of bone and muscle and blood, I sense a kind of inner northern-lights play of flow and space. I open my awareness wider than if I were focusing on a task that I know how to do. I embrace and boogie with not knowing, turning toward the wordless places inside as I lightly float my consciousness toward an idea or a project I'm interested in at the moment. My sense of physicality shifts to champagne-like bubbles of streaming sensation in my blood. Time disappears in the midst of creating, and there is actually no "me" in the process. I just feel the delicious fountain flow that sometimes trickles and sometimes gushes.

I alternate between actual sensation and sensing the next step. Imagine holding something you know in one hand and the unknown in the other. Imagine tossing and juggling the known and the unknown just as you would balls or balloons. Remember the fun and the flow of doing that as a child. Creating can give you that playful inner experience anytime.

When we've asked our students and colleagues to describe how creating feels for them, they've shared some similar experiences. Dee, a minister and animal activist, says:

I feel an effervescing bubbling of ideas and possibilities. An expanding synergy of movement gathering momentum that simultaneously has upward expansion and downward grounding. I also feel a loss of limitations of time, space, rules, etc.

Lynn, a professional artist, describes her experience of creating this way:

Creating takes me out of the fear trance immediately. As soon as I begin, I am aware of possibilities, and fear melts. I feel easy, joyful, excited, energized, and totally present in the moment.

Carey, an architect and designer, experiences a sense of time-less engagement that transcends ordinary limits:

> When I create, time goes away. Four hours seems like five minutes. I am focused *and* spacious, moving *and* still, here *and* away, solving *and* meditating. I feel present and alive. I am existing in the space between, where life takes place. Nothing else matters.

Jody, a coach and improvisation specialist, describes her inner experience of creating:

> When creating, my body feels like a silent motor is on, a gentle, lifting whirring accompanied by a laser-clear yet gentle focus and lots of subtle movement in my body. I feel a heightened sense of presence with what is there and what is coming into my awareness.

As you can see, creating builds a satisfying and fulfilling inner experience regardless of the particular outcome—the dish or the new strategy or the work of art. The fact that it feels so good also causes a big problem that human beings have been struggling with for a long time.

How Does Creative Flow Turn into Fear?

Much of humanity suffers from a prohibition against enjoying genuine, organic good feeling of any kind for any extended period of time. Unfortunately, that "extended period of time" is often only a matter of ten seconds or less. Being in touch with one's creative essence is so powerful and life changing that it scares many people off. They fear that something bad will happen if they open up a direct connection to the creative part of themselves.

What, actually, is the fear based on? We've put a lot of research into that question, both in our own lives and in the lives of the people we've worked with. Much of it is driven by fear of the unknown, something that humans have been wrestling with from time immemorial. Creativity by its very nature has a big element of the unknown in it. Creativity has to surprise you with something new; otherwise, it's not creativity, it's just a rearrangement of thoughts from the past. Also, many people have told us they feared that opening up fully to their creative essence would somehow make them irresponsible or, at worst, some sort of mad genius who lived alone in the forest.

In our seminars, we invite the participants to inquire deeply into their own stories to discover the reasons they can't access their creativity fully. As you hear one after another of their stories, you begin to realize that they're all the same story. It goes like this: Something happens in our lives to disrupt our connection with our creative essences, perhaps the chaos of our parents divorcing or the death of a precious loved one. Then we cover up the pain of losing our creative connection by hurling ourselves, consciously or unconsciously, into something that is ultimately destructive. Maybe it's alcohol, cigarettes, or other drugs. Maybe it's binge eating or binge television or binge romance. We've used most of those destructive habits ourselves, as well as hearing clients tell us about dozens of other "weapons of mass distraction," as one of them put it. At their core, all of them are the same: their purpose is to distract us from the pain and emptiness of losing contact with the creative spirit inside us.

Most of us haven't actually known a mad genius who has to live alone in the woods. We might have seen one on television or in the movies. It doesn't matter: Our minds are the best moviemaking machines ever created! The mind is particularly gifted at making short horror clips. Given a squirt of adrenaline from some fear in your belly about the first-ever speech you're about to give, your own personal movie studio will be happy to manufacture a two-minute trailer of your own personal thriller/horror film. You'll see such gripping sequences as the audience sprinting for the exits with fingers in their ears after your opening line. You'll watch yourself being booed off the stage or choking on the poorly cooked chicken you forced yourself to eat while waiting for your speech to begin. All those sequences are made up by your mind, fueled by the fear in your belly.

In the same way, our minds crank out justifications, manufactured by the scared part of us, to support our daily choice to stay in the rut of routine rather than risking the unknown life outside the rut. The rut may be dull, boring, and bereft of passion, but it holds an enduring grip on us because it's *familiar*. Personally, we're far too well acquainted with that particular rut. We've been there ourselves—you surely have too—and we do not want to go back there ever again. It took a lot of work and talking and love and forgiveness—sometimes taking one step forward and then sliding two steps back—to get our creativity back on the line and rebirth our relationship at midlife.

The merry-go-round of relationship routine and the pull of the familiar become particularly challenging at midlife and beyond. When travelers discovered salt and spices centuries ago, food preparation entered an entirely new and exciting phase that continues to this day. Relationships require spices too. Since humans all crave variety along with comfortable ritual, people often resort to unconscious disruptions to spice up the familiar when relating has become bland. Flirtations, addictions, Internet roaming, Facebook flings, and more provide a spicy zing in ways that erode intimacy and true co-creativity. In contrast, when you commit to create and renew yourself, you generate zesty variety in your communication, invitations to connect, and choices to grow and challenge yourself, all of which deepen intimacy and enhance attractiveness.

Belly Trumps Brain . . . Unless

The emotional part of our brains is huge compared to the thinking part. In actual physical dimensions, it's about the difference in size between the juicy part of a grapefruit and the rind. The thinking mind is the rind, the most recent part of our brains to develop. It takes conscious work on ourselves to get the juicy parts of ourselves into harmony with the thinking parts.

Given the movie-making skills of the mind, it's easy to take our fears seriously. The squeak of a floorboard can set off a mental movie sequence of a monster in the basement. Of course, sometimes there actually *is* a monster in the basement, but the statistics are on your side. What we all need to do is retrain ourselves so we get scared about the things we really need to get scared about—what we really ought to fight against or run from—and not about the things that contain no actual threat to us.

For example, Gay had the habit in his 20s and 30s of unconsciously projecting images of the dad he never knew onto male authority figures, leading to anger and disappointment when they inevitably fulfilled the dictates of the script. Gay says, "Once I realized where the projector was located, I suddenly had a choice I didn't recognize before. I could unplug it or I could run a better quality movie on it, but I didn't just have to keep watching the same movie over and over again!"

The emotion of fear is more changeable than most people think. One of the wisest and most useful bits of wisdom we've ever received came from Fritz Perls, M.D.: fear is excitement without the breath. The same mechanisms that run fear also run excitement, but if you constrict your breathing, the unpleasant sensations of fear kick in. The more you constrict, the more scared you feel. Finally, when you remember to breathe fully in participation with the moment, you can actually feel fear turn into excitement in your body. Usually three or four easy, deep breaths will help you tell if there is a real monster in the basement or just some neglected exercise equipment your brain is madly thinking up reasons not to use!

Many people also worry that opening to their creative essence will disrupt their routines. No need to worry: it will. However, when it's finished disrupting your routines, you'll probably join us in saying some version of "Thank goodness!" In a few moments we're going to suggest a small conscious change in your routines. From it, you will likely reap such a remarkable burst of new energy in your love life that you may wonder, as we did, *Why haven't I been doing this all along?* It's that good. Of course, there's only one way to find that out, and that's to give it a sincere implementation.

Your Move

Here's how to get the process started: It begins with a commitment, the same one we made ourselves, the same one we teach in our seminars. The commitment will open the gateway for you to learn, rapidly and easily, things that took us years to learn by trial and error. The commitment takes pain out of the learning process, making positive change happen gently and rapidly.

Here's the commitment:

I commit to enjoying my full capacity for love and creativity.

Right where you are, try out that sentence a few times in your mind or aloud. Get the feel of it. Say it out loud and listen to the vibration of the word-sounds in the air. Breathe with it. Savor it in every way you can. Find out if it's a commitment you can embrace sincerely. There's no pressure. It's your choice.

Take a moment to understand the idea behind the commitment. A commitment is a stand you take. In this case you're taking a stand for a certain kind of enjoyment. You're choosing to take joy in the experience of more creativity and love in your life.

As you consider this commitment, imagine that you have a Sincere-O-Meter that can measure how sincere you are about a given commitment. Your Sincere-O-Meter measures how fully your body and soul are committed to producing a successful outcome. For example, if you commit to going to the pharmacy to get medicine for a sick child, how likely are you to stop off at a tavern or video arcade along the way?

What does your imaginary Sincere-O-Meter tell you about how much you're engaged, body and soul, in the process of generating more creativity and love in your life? There are no right or wrong answers to that question; it's often more a matter of timing than anything else. Is this the right time for you to make a major commitment to expanding your connection to your creative essence? Is this the right time for you to focus on growing more love in your life?

For example, sometimes, if you're single, you need to be focusing on the experience of being by yourself more than you need to be focusing on relating to another person. The same thing is true for couples. Sometimes you are so focused on finding the money to pay for the kids' orthodontia that you don't feel you have the energy to add one more thing, even if it's something that could save your marriage or possibly your life.

One reason this commitment—when you're ready to make it—is so liberating is that it wipes out all your past history of suffering in the name of love and creativity. When you make a commitment to enjoying more love and creativity, you're saying to the world (and to yourself) that you intend to create joy, rather than suffering, in the two most important areas of your life.

For us, it was a revelation to discover that suffering was not an absolute requirement in either of these areas. We both grew up around close family members who tortured themselves and those in the vicinity through the mistaken impression that nicotine, alcohol, and other drugs were required to feed their creativity. Chaos followed.

Fortunately we discovered that chemicals are not required and that suffering is only one option. Both love and creativity can grow every day with ease and fun rather than pain and drama. In the early part of our lives, we thought pain and drama were fundamental requirements—the way relationships had to be. We now call that a classic example of taking a "frog's-eye" view of the situation. Frogs can only see things that have a few specific qualities: the item has to be small, black, and moving, otherwise the frog can't see it. Even if the Rose Bowl parade is going by in front of a frog, the frog can't see a thing, unless some flies happen to be buzzing around the bands. Flies are what frogs like to look at best. For the last 65 million years or so since flies first appeared in the fossil record, frogs have loved to eat flies so much that nature, in its efficient wisdom, has arranged it so that the frog doesn't even have to look at anything else! In that same way, our frog's-eye view from early childhood was that relationships required constant suffering and compromise. We had no idea that just outside our limited vision, a whole Rose Bowl parade of better possibilities was marching by.

Go for the parade. Choose the new possibility now. Bring it into form with the new commitment we're suggesting:

I commit to enjoying my full capacity for love and creativity.

Keep circulating the commitment through your consciousness as we move along. Say the words and feel the sincerity of your commitment in your body. Appreciate yourself for doing this remarkable thing: you're bringing a new state of consciousness into being through the power of your commitment. If you're newly discovering that power in your life, consider yourself fortunate indeed. The act of making and keeping big, meaningful agreements with yourself is the cornerstone of well-being.

Turning Toward Consciousness

When you encounter any problem in life, one good way to start solving it is to ask yourself these questions: How have I gotten out of harmony with my inner tuning fork? How have I lost touch with my creative essence? Close love relationships often stifle this essence in the participants, so that after being together for a while they are less creative than they were before they met. Check this out in your own awareness right now. Have you had the experience of feeling less and less creative and less engaged and alive as a relationship progressed?

We were in our mid-40s when we first began to wake up to this problem. Looking back to where we were 20 years ago, we find it almost horrifying to contemplate how much of our precious creative energy was being eaten up by recycled squabbles and the low-level background noise of bickering. Once we discovered there were other items on the menu besides suffering, we never had the urge to go back. We found that we were able to make a home in a new place we'd never dreamed existed. You can live there too. It's just a matter of dedication.

Consider the commitment again:

I commit to enjoying my full capacity for love and creativity.

Focus in again on the *enjoying* aspect of the commitment. In our experience, creativity is a totally positive thing. We want it to be that way for you too. In our view, the world has had plenty of suffering in the name of creativity. For example, think of the suffering of Mozart, penniless and freezing as he composed note after note, dedicated to his art to his last dying breath. It wasn't the suffering that made his music great; it was his natural gifts, daily practice, and a constant dedication to transcending himself.

For many people, especially those who have experienced great pain in love, it's difficult to conceive of expanding in love without also expanding into more pain. Your new commitment solves that problem with a specific intention to *enjoy* your full capacity for love.

If you are willing to make the commitment sincerely from your heart, you create something new and very useful, much like the tuning note sounded at the beginning of a symphony concert. Orchestras usually tune to the A note played on an oboe, because that particular note on that particular instrument is easiest to keep in tune. The sound of this tone has two immediate effects: The other musicians in the orchestra tune to the A until they reach a harmonious whole. At the same time, the audience hears the harmonious whole coming together and another tuning occurs as they focus their consciousness on the freshly harmonized orchestra.

Commitment works like that. When you make a sincere commitment, you sound a new tone in your consciousness, like the oboe's A at the beginning of a concert. Then the rest of your being can begin to harmonize with the new ideas contained in the commitment. When the oboe player blows that A, it makes a statement to the orchestra: "Here is a way for us individuals to become a harmonious whole. Will you join me?" Your commitment works the same way. You sound the new tone—*I commit to enjoying my full capacity for love and creativity*—and then you allow the rest of your being to tune to it.

Deeper into Commitment

The commitment we're working with—*I commit to enjoying my full capacity for love and creativity*—contains three powerful concepts. Any of the three concepts has the power on its own to change your life, but putting them all together synergizes that power into something much stronger. Think for a moment about the amazing new life path you are opening up for yourself when you make the commitment:

- First, you take a conscious stand for enjoyment, the experience of being *in joy* as you go about the crucial task of expanding the love and creativity in your life. Vowing to *enjoy* your learning about love and creativity, rather than suffering with it, sends powerful messages to your inner self. The messages say, *I intend to stop replaying the old dramas. I intend now to focus on the present, on the actual experience of enjoying more love and creativity in my life. I'm here for joy.* These messages open up a new world inside you, a vast universe of new space you can fill with joyful sensations.

- Second, you are taking a conscious stand to grow your capacity for love. "All time not spent on love is wasted," says the philosopher Tasso, and 35 years of relationship counseling have confirmed that truth for us. By making the commitment, you're saying to your deepest self, "I'm here to grow the love in my life. I want to feel the most love I possibly can. I hereby dedicate myself to going all the way in feeling loved and loving. I'm here *for love."*

- Third, you take a conscious stand for your creativity. A quick look around you will probably confirm what we've observed: not very many people are expressing their creative passions in life. You step into rarified territory when you make a deliberate choice in favor of your creativity. It's like learning to breathe a new and better form of oxygen; it takes some getting used to. It might even feel lonely at first, until you realize there are a lot of people out in the world doing the same thing you're doing: recovering their inner joy, feeling love and creativity expanding in their lives every day. After seeing thousands of people use the tools in this book to transform their relationships, we've never seen anyone who was remotely tempted to go back to the old adrenaline-fueled dramas of the past.

The Creativity One-Step

Now it's time to focus on how to bring your commitment to life in your daily activities.

Float the commitment through your awareness again:

I commit to enjoying my full capacity for love and creativity.

By taking a stand to *enjoy* a major expansion of the *love* and *creativity* you feel every day, you set in motion a huge life change. It's so big that you need a single, simple step you can take every day. You need a focal point: a solid, reliable way to put the commitment to work for you.

In our work with the relationships of people 45 and older, we have discovered this single, simple step. It would probably be useful at any age, but because of creativity's importance for those in relationships after age 45, it can be a life saver as well as a relationship saver.

Here's what you can do every day to demonstrate your commitment to expanding to your full capacity for love and creativity: do your creativity first!

Begin each day by engaging with one of your creative passions, if only for ten minutes, *before* you engage with e-mail, the Internet, or anything related to other kinds of work. We have found that ten minutes of creative work is the minimum. It doesn't sound like much, but it's enough to send a new message to your inner self: my creative work is a high priority for me.

This action step is a way to make clear to yourself and the people around you that you are sincere about growing the love and creativity you feel in your life. Why? Because you are putting the highest priority on practicing your creativity, doing something that you love to do regardless of its productive value. Doing creativity first—and combining it with love—sets the tone for your day and for the kind of life you want to live.

For example, Katie describes her morning creative practice:

I gently stretch while giving my loving attention to any tight spots in my body. Then I pull out my notebook and open it on the floor. As a kinesthetic learner, I've noticed over the years that moving ignites my wondering and creates connections that just thinking doesn't. I let my body tell me whether I want to stand, sit, or lie down, and then I listen to the impulses to move as they arise from my foot or back or hip. I simply follow those as far as the impulse wants to travel, then settle back into actively listening for the next impulse. It's like spreading out a blanket on a meadow and enjoying a picnic of the best delicacies at the perfect pace.

I might find a shape or rhythm that I toss to different limbs, or I make the movement much bigger or much smaller. My intention is to give awareness to moving and to move from the inside out, kind of a movement stream of consciousness. Often during my ten minutes of moving, ideas, new processes, and entire projects pop up in my mind. I jot these down in my notebook and go back to moving.

My notebook is filled with creative possibilities, many of which have become online courses, books, and seminars, and it feels like a treasure to open every day. When you start every day with ten minutes doing something you love to do that makes time disappear, you generate a creative template for the day that makes everything else easier and more fun.

When we talk about this point in a lecture, hands invariably go up in the auditorium right about now: "Hold on! What if my kids wake up sick? Are you suggesting that I go write a poem before I take care of them?" No, of course not. Handle emergencies first. However, the dishes can probably wait. For Katie, the spotless kitchen was a big barrier:

> I found it hard to break my addiction to making sure everything was spotless before I'd allow myself to do any of my creative work. The first few days of putting my creativity first were hard. The whole time I was doing my creative work I kept thinking of all the stuff that needed doing. After a few days, though, I got the big surge of positive energy that made it all worthwhile. Putting my creativity first also helped me learn how to delegate tasks to other people, instead of doing my martyr act and thinking I had to do everything myself.

The idea of putting your creativity first is so radical that the mind will usually start firing off a fusillade of reasons why it's absolutely impossible for you to do it. By the time we get to midlife, as we've said, many of us have lost touch with our creative essence, and human beings feel despair when they lose touch with that precious part of themselves. To keep us from feeling the pain of that loss in its pure, unadulterated form, our minds try to drown out the despair with an infinite number of justifications. We don't have time, we've got too many responsibilities, we're just too tired. All of those and more went through our own minds as we got our new routine established.

One of the beautiful things about the human mind is that eventually it tends to gravitate toward a better idea. Celebrating your creativity every day is obviously a much better idea than squelching it or letting it lie fallow. Even so, it took us quite a few faltering steps before we faithfully committed to our creativity first every day. That's why we recommend putting your creativity first for three days in a row. It helps you get it rooted as a habit in your life.

You never know how long a commitment will take to produce observable results, but it's best to let go of expectations. The main reason to let go of expectations is that change often happens faster than people expect. If you're not used to the power of clearly expressed commitments, you may be surprised at how quickly things change right after you express a sincere commitment. We learned that right away in ourselves, and we certainly confirmed it with our clients and seminar students.

For example, we worked with a couple, Andrea and Roger, in a long marriage that had gone dull after years of wrestling with the same problems over and over. After their first session, which mostly consisted of a deep experience of the Love Catalyst for Couples (which you'll find in Appendix A), they thanked us and made an appointment for a month later. When they came back, we could hardly believe our eyes. For one thing, Andrea looked 30 pounds lighter and radiantly healthy in a yellow sundress. The last time we'd seen her, she'd been dressed in baggy clothes and her face had had an unhealthy pallor, the "library tan" of the professional academic she was. Roger's forehead, which had been furrowed with worry wrinkles the month before, was now relatively smooth. He looked like a burden had been lifted off him.

It turned out that Andrea hadn't gone on an official diet. "I just stopped eating sugar and the weight fell off by itself," she said. Roger had come by his forehead the natural way too. He summed up the discovery: "After we left here last time, we pulled off the road and talked for a long time. We both realized we'd said good-bye to our own individual creativity the day we got married twenty years ago." Andrea said, "It was like we made a deal with each other when we got married—if you don't grow or change, I won't either." Roger said, "It wasn't a good deal. It was killing us."

"So, what exactly did you do?" we asked.

"Just what you suggested," Andrea replied. "We put our creativity first. I started journaling again. I do it for a little while every morning, anywhere from ten minutes to half an hour."

Roger, a businessman, said, "For me it's mostly sketching out ideas on paper, playing with new ways of putting things together, but the big thing was doing it first, before I start answering e-mail and doing other routine stuff. That made me start waking up with creative ideas instead of waking up dreading all the stuff on my to-do list."

There are plenty of other big ideas you'll learn as we move along through the book, but imbue this first one with a special aura:

When we human beings get into deeper harmony with our own creative essence, our relationships blossom. When we don't, they don't. People who are alive to their inner flow, who listen to and resonate with the inner tuning fork of their creativity, become available for co-creativity. They receive life and let daily experiences expand their discoveries and choices with the people around them. Harmony only happens between two or more separate notes. When harmony in music emerged in the Renaissance, a revolution of possibilities emerged. You can let harmony emerge in your love life by committing to your creativity and being open to co-creating with your beloved. You're constantly expanding your experience of creative flow and new possibilities, so that each interaction with others becomes a new experiment in generating harmony. Picture two full, whole voices blending and creating throughout life. That's what your creative commitment and practice can become.

This kind of creativity can make everyday miracles happen. A colleague of ours describes a process he and his wife invented by playing with new creative choices:

> Here's one of my favorite shift moves with my hot wife. When things are going downhill fast, one of us will request a "do-over." And literally, we'll start over. For example, I'll walk outside the door, and open the door again and say, "Honey, I'm home!" in a cheerful voice. We can't help laughing, and the upset is over. As another example, I once said something less than sweet as we were falling asleep in bed. She was feeling hurt, and I wanted to create a shift in our connection and feel close again. So I held out my hand and said, "Give it back."

"I can't . . . the damage has been done. It's too late," she replied dramatically.

"Come on . . . give it back . . ." and we became more playful. When my wife did give it back, I immediately got out of bed, walked directly to the toilet, and flushed it down. There's something about the do-over that we use to reliably create a shift.

We *know* that a commitment to creativity has the power to work miracles. It certainly did so with our colleague and his wife, with Andrea and Roger, and with thousands more of our clients, as well as for us; we wouldn't have the relationship we do if we both didn't practice this step diligently in our own lives, every day. Will it work for you? There's a quick way to find out.

Small Change, Big Miracle

Take this one simple step to get the flow of miracles going:

Starting tomorrow, do at least ten minutes of exploration with your most important creative project first—before you do routine things like e-mail, household tasks, and errands. An hour or two with your creativity would probably be great, but our research has found that it's got to be minimally ten minutes. Then, if you do that same thing again the next day and the next, you've established a trend. We've found that that's what it takes to get the new pattern rooted in your awareness.

While it's only a tiny alteration in your routine, it sets in motion big, positive changes throughout your life. In our own case, those changes took us to places we'd never known existed, new heights of intimacy we'd never imagined possible. Now, it's become part of our overall life purpose to share what we've learned about the relationship between creativity and your love life. As we go along you'll learn about the miracles we've seen when people at midlife and beyond make choices in favor of their creativity. We're very passionate about this subject, and you may hear an urgency in our voice about this matter. That's because in addition to the miracles we've seen, we've also seen the unhappy consequences when people at midlife and beyond choose not to heed the sound of creativity calling.

Sledgehammer or Feather: Pick One

Like us, you've had painful experiences in the area of love. Some of those events probably felt like sledgehammers; you got hit with a shocking amount of reality in a very short period of time. In counseling couples over the years, we've heard dozens of versions of one common sledgehammer moment, the one when you hear your partner tell you, "I've been having an affair." At the time you experience those moments, they seem to come out of nowhere. It was only in looking back over them that we began to see a life-altering truth emerge: before every one of those sledgehammer moments, people had tuned out a series of cues that were giving them progressively larger hints about the matter. It's as if the universe has a special feature built into it, a device that tickles us with a feather several times to get our attention about something we need to pay attention to. If we don't respond to the feather tickles, the universe goes sledgehammer on us.

After experiencing a number of sledgehammer moments of our own, we finally came to a realization that changed our lives even more profoundly: it was always our own hand on the handle of the hammer! We came to call this the Upper Limit Problem, as we mentioned in the Introduction—the universal tendency of human beings to sabotage ourselves when we begin to experience more love, success, or positive energy in general. You can get more detail about the Upper Limit Problem in Gay's book *The Big Leap*, but here are the essentials you need to know right now.

Fear drives the Upper Limit Problem. To understand why we humans persist in sabotaging ourselves when we start to rise in love or wealth or anything positive, we need to put the spotlight of awareness on several specific fears. Probably the most common fear we've encountered, in ourselves and in working with others, is a fear that we are inadequate in some unnamed way, that we are fundamentally flawed, undeserving of love and happiness. There are other fears too, such as a fear of outshining other people, a reticence in showing our own gifts so as not to make others feel diminished.

The Upper Limit Problem works the same way for singles and for couples, and it often operates in more dramatic fashion at midlife and beyond. Now that we've had 20 years of opportunity to study midlife and older relationships, certain key truths have emerged. One truth is this: whatever patterns have been limiting you before midlife—whether known to you or concealed from conscious awareness—will begin to appear in more and more obvious, almost cartoonlike form after midlife. For example, we worked with a man we'll call Phil who came in for his first-ever session of relationship coaching with a lifetime story of loss and betrayal. From his teenage years to midlife he had suffered through more than a dozen women leaving him, sometimes after a few weeks, sometimes after a couple of years. After we heard the story, we asked him what had caused him to seek help for the issue now. He said, "Recently I've begun to wonder if it could have something to do with *me*."

That's what we mean when we say that after midlife the old patterns often come to your attention with a cartoonlike quality. If, for whatever reason, conscious or unconscious, we decide to ignore some important issue when we're 30 or 40, it's bound to come back in a more compelling form in our 50s. The same goes for important things we choose to ignore at 50 or 60: expect a return engagement with them in the next decade or so. In one way or another we all have the same problem Phil had. We keep repeating an old pattern, unaware that it's a pattern, to a point when we suddenly snap out of the trance we've been in and think, *Hmmm, could this possibly have something to do with me?*

Browsing YouTube once, we found a classic film sequence of the old-time comedian W. C. Fields. In it, Fields is trying to take a nap on his back porch swing. First a milkman disturbs his rest; next, an erratically rolling coconut. The more he tries to shut the outside world out, the more preposterous the interruptions become. Finally, all possibilities of a nap end when a man on the street below starts repeatedly bellowing out the name "Carl LaFong." If you're like us, you probably don't get up off the sofa the first few times you hear the knock on the door. Eventually you respond, though, if only to relieve the pain of the persistent noise. At midlife and beyond, things bang on the door a lot louder. There's an urgency—you've got a lot less time to deal with the important stuff.

The place to start exploring the Upper Limit Problem is at home, inside ourselves and in our closest relationships. Ultimately you will likely come to the realization that the deepest fear human beings must somehow get through is the fear of our own magnificence. It's said that the big human fear is death, but by and large, people seem to deal with death pretty well. Given the gravity of the situation we all face in that regard, it's remarkable we don't see people running down the street every day in a panic yelling, "I'm going to die. You're going to die. We're all going to die!"

In our experience, the fear of our own magnificence—our love and creativity in full bloom—occupies a great deal more of our conscious and unconscious bandwidth than the fear of death. It's a crucial life issue, the question of whether or not we will liberate our full capacity for love and creativity within our lifetimes. Right alongside that fear is another emotion that people often feel at midlife and beyond: a sense of despair that the ship may have already sailed, that your possibilities for love and creative fulfillment are behind you. If you've felt any of that fear and despair, we've been there too. Ultimately, though, we realized that all the fear came with a rainbow behind it.

The Rainbow Behind All the Fear

The rainbow behind the fear has a very different message to it. The fear says, "It isn't possible to express your full potential for love and creativity in this world. And even if it were possible, it wouldn't be safe." Behind the fear, a different message is written on the rainbow: "Fulfilling your potential is not only possible, it's the only way to find true safety in this world."

We want you to feel that true safety and bring it to life in the heart of your relationships. We've had the privilege for many years of seeing people move through their fears and find their home in the rainbow of their full potential. We've seen the radiance on the faces of a 75-year-old couple as they broke through to a new level of intimacy after 50 years together. We've seen the miracle of a 55-year-old getting out of a long-term abusive relationship and creating a loving marriage with a partner who adores her.

We've been privileged to live on a steady diet of those miracles for a long time now, so we have plenty of stories to share with you. The next chapter begins with one of the most remarkable ones we've ever seen: how a ten-second communication broke a four-year orgasmic drought.

By now we hope we've convinced you that opening up a deeper flow of connection with your creativity will help you discover a greater flow of love inside you and around you. Keep that idea front and center in your awareness as we proceed.

Moving Forward

The enigmatic Yogi Berra once said, "When you come to a fork in the road, take it." We'd like to add a little more detail to Yogi's suggestion, based on the sum total of our work with midlife-and-beyond relationships: when you come to any impasse in your relationship life, it's an opportunity to open more to your own creative essence. As you open the flow of that connection to the creative wellspring within you, miracles begin to happen in your love life, "as if by magic." It won't be magic that makes it happen, though. It will be your commitment and your diligence that make it happen (assisted by some simple, ingenious tools we'll describe to you).

It's time to move forward now in learning those tools. Get centered in your commitment and bring it to life as a benign marching order:

I commit to enjoying my full capacity for love and creativity!

Then make a solemn vow to yourself to put that commitment to work tomorrow by honoring the creative imperative: do at least a little bit of your creative practice first, before you get into the other business of your day. Play with colors on paper, sing your ideas out loud, collage or doodle on a whiteboard. Whether you reinvent your favorite soup or rearrange pieces of a poem in a sketchbook, your creative process gives priority to what you so love to do that time disappears when you dive into your morning practice.

Once you start to reconnect with your creative essence, miracles happen, as we've said. And if you want some specific guidelines for bringing your creative energy to bear on the way you relate to your partner, in Appendix A you'll find we've included the key activity we use ourselves and with clients to enjoy creativity and co-creativity in our daily relating. The title itself may give away its purpose—The Genius of Relationship Process: Liberating Your Hidden Creativity. Creativity replaces habitual patterns with play and possibility, which can become the backdrop for more daily joy for you and for your close relationships.

That's all you need to do to get the journey under way. The next chapter shows you how to keep your capacity for love and creativity growing through the speed bumps and detours that life tends to serve up. Caution: we'll describe some moments that made our palms sweat when we lived through them, whether we were experiencing them ourselves or listening with our hearts wide open during counseling sessions. If you experience any perspiration from reading about these adventures, whether it's a profane word or a strong image that gets your autonomic system humming, it's probably a good thing. It shows you're emotionally involved in making good on your commitment to enjoying your full capacity for love and creativity. That's what we want, and we bet it's what you want in your own deepest heart of hearts.

If that's as true for you as it is for us, let's explore another level of magic that awaits, something we can hardly wait to tell you about, something we discovered in our 50s at a deeper and more profound level than we had ever known before. It's something we think should be chiseled on the outside of public buildings right alongside "Ye shall know the truth . . ."

It's three little words you don't see together very often.

CHAPTER TWO

Integrity Is Sexy

Sexy? Did we say integrity is *sexy*? Yes, integrity is sexier than just about anything you can get your hands on, as you will soon see.

It's not only sexy, it's simple and easy. Instead of simple and easy, though, we humans manage to make it mighty complicated and hard at times. How we have managed to take such a simple thing as integrity and complicate it so maddeningly is a subject for a whole book, but the bottom line is this: what makes integrity simple and easy is also what makes it so hard; what makes it so hard is also what makes it so sexy.

For most people, sex is not the first thing that comes to mind when they think of integrity. But integrity isn't a moral issue—it's an energy issue. Choosing integrity aligns the flow of feeling, sensation, and communication inside so your creativity moves through you unimpeded. Consider this definition of integrity: "an unbroken wholeness or totality with nothing wanting." Imagine feeling clear, present, and available all the time in your life and relationships. Imagine making daily choices at work and with others openly and freely. Imagine having no secrets and no hidden feelings or communications. Integrity, your wholeness, can be accessed, recovered, and treasured throughout life.

We've included a complete description of integrity skills in Appendix B, but here are the basics. When you live in your wholeness, you do what you say you're going to do and you don't do what you say you're not going to do. You're aware of your feelings and can speak about them easily so others understand. You listen deeply and generously to others and speak in a way that closely matches your inner experience. You can reliably shift from blame to wonder and immediately claim ownership of any issues that arise in your life while inviting others to claim their ability to generate solutions and collaboration. You generate appreciation rather than complaint and criticism and see others, especially those close to you, as whole, resourceful, and creative.

This list may sound like wishful thinking, but in our decades of exploring and teaching integrity skills, we've found that people can harmonize their actions to their inner tuning fork, choice by choice. Each move to align your words with your feelings, and your actions with authenticity, produces more energy and vibrance. Integrity makes your skin glow, your breath deepen, your eyes sparkle with discovery. And *that's* incredibly sexy.

Consider how most integrity problems wouldn't take even ten seconds to fix. From our files: Marty had a sexual encounter with his partner's best friend, but neither of them has told Marty's partner. All Marty and the best friend need to do is make a brief communication. They could say something simple, "We had sex," and still have most of the ten seconds left over.

Bill Clinton had a famous ten-second integrity problem, but being steeped in the conventional political and legal wisdom of lying and denying, he stretched it out for months until DNA caught him out. It's hard to imagine what might have happened if he'd used his ten-second window to say, "Yes, I actually did have sexual relations with Miss Lewinsky." However, no matter how much the citizenry might have recoiled from hearing an actual unvarnished truth from a politician, it could hardly have been worse than the year that followed the famous integrity breach.

In our seminars and our office, we've been present to many moments in which someone said the equivalent of "Yes, I actually did have sex with _____." The ten seconds of raw postconfession emotion after such moments are just as important as the ten seconds of the confession itself. It's usually anger and sadness that pour forth, sometimes expressed at high volume and using words that are wincingly base. However unpleasant the emotions are at the time, they always serve a positive purpose. They are always steps in the direction of positive evolution for the relationship.

Here we must insert a giant caveat: it never does any good to have the same loud argument over and over. What does couples a great deal of good is to get underneath the recycling argument to the raw fears and grief that are the hidden drivers of the never-ending conflict. Those raw expressions of feeling, if facilitated well, seldom last longer than a matter of minutes. Holding secret or unexpressed feelings is like putting a fist around your inner tuning fork and dampening the tone so that it sputters rather than vibrating through you with clarity. Later in the book we'll give you clear instructions for your Ten-Minute Heart Talk, which will include suggestions on moving through emotions gently and smoothly and using integrity skills to come into harmony with your whole self again.

Getting the Integrity Wobbles

So, the thing that makes integrity so simple and easy is also the reason why we spend so much time slipping out of integrity and trying to get back in. Think of how easy it is to go out of integrity! Given that, it's a miracle we humans don't spend our lives in a perpetual integrity wobble. To go out of integrity, all we need to do is say one little thing that isn't true. Actually, it's even easier: all we need to do is *think* one little thing that isn't true. If we really want to take our integrity wobble to the extreme, we can do something we don't want the world to know about and then lie to hide it.

It's extremely easy *not* to tell your mate about your affair with the best friend. For a while, at least, it's easier to hide it and mask the wobble than it is to restore integrity and steady yourself. However, life does not let us off the hook like that. For the 98 percent of us humans who aren't psychopaths, it eventually becomes hard to maintain the wobble. Being out of integrity makes us miserable, sick, and distant from our committed beloveds. Finally we can't stand it anymore and we reveal ourselves.

Unfortunately, we often reveal ourselves through some unconscious means such as an accident or illness. The crisis forces the truth to the surface, and integrity is restored. In our files are several examples from people who waited until after a heart attack, when they didn't know if they would live or die, to reveal a long-withheld truth. In one extreme situation the truth was "I have a wife and kids in Chicago I've never told you about. That's where I go on my sales trips." According to the widow who shared the story with us, she had felt something strange was going on in their relationship for a long time. Whenever she brought up the subject, though, her husband always stonewalled her with a response like "You're too sensitive. Everything's fine."

Come into a session with us, so you can see what one of those extreme examples looks like up close:

Enter Clara, 49, accompanied by her husband of 30 years, Rodney, 51. She is bespectacled and modestly dressed; we know from her intake form she's a health professional with a long and distinguished career. He's the picture of a prosperous businessman, dressed in a power suit, his tie casually loosened for the occasion.

During the next hour a great many things are discussed, but the climax of the session is one ten-second utterance by Clara. That sentence charges the energy in the room as fast as the crack of lightning that starts the storm. Rodney snaps upright and a heat rush floods his cheeks. That night they go home and make wild, passionate love. Clara has her first orgasm in four years.

What was the sentence Clara spoke that led to such a bone-shuddering, satisfying conclusion?

It was a sentence that brought her into a state of integrity. She spoke a few words, and those words made a difference in her body. After being out of integrity for four years, her body was ripe to rejoice in its restoration.

It was a sentence that restored integrity in two ways, the ordinary and the extraordinary. The ordinary way of thinking about integrity is in moral terms: something has integrity if it fits the established definition of morality. When Clara spoke her ten seconds of orgasm-producing integrity, she acted in a moral way according to her standards. She lifted a burden off herself in the release of the guilt she'd been carrying. When Clara spoke her magic sentence, it restored wholeness to herself and to her marriage. At the same time, her action demonstrated the definition of integrity we call extraordinary: integrity, as we said, is about *wholeness*. Unlike the moral way of looking at integrity, this is pure physics.

Okay, let's end the suspense. Here's what Clara said that led to the restoration of ecstatic sex in her relationship with Rodney after a four-year drought:

"I had sex with your best friend four years ago."

We've witnessed many truths revealed over the years, but that one pegged the meter. It set off a thunderstorm of heated communication, which included some telling details, an eruption of anger and sadness from Rodney, and questions about how they both could have gotten so distant from each other. Rodney began wondering about his own unexpressed truths, such as using long work hours to avoid facing his decreased sexual interest in Clara. This very fast ping-pong exchange of withheld communications was finally followed by a long, sobbing hug at the end. Later, though, they discovered the ecstatic payoff for their courage in doing all that difficult emotional work. In each other's arms they found a depth of release that had eluded them for four years, the exact amount of time that the withheld communication had gotten its stranglehold on the flow of intimacy between them.

Here's why integrity can produce such miraculous results:

Integrity problems in relationships drain energy and destroy intimacy. Broken promises, untold truths, concealed feelings—these are all problems of integrity that erode love and trust in relationships. On the positive side, though, fixing an integrity problem can restore the flow of good feeling so fast it still astonishes us. Even though we've witnessed it hundreds of times now, we're still moved by the healing power of a few simple integrity moves. The good news: the integrity skills that make intimacy flourish take ten seconds or less to do.

Here's a brief bit of dialogue from our first session with a 50-something couple, Barbara and Art.

> Barbara: We haven't been really fighting or anything, but something just feels "off" between us.

> Art: And no matter how many times I tell her everything's fine, she's never satisfied.

> Barbara: See? There it is right there—according to him everything's always "fine."

> Art: Can't you for once just be satisfied with things being fine?

Have you ever had a conversation like that?

Early in our marriage we had plenty of them. It took Gay a couple of years to stop playing Art's role and start treating Katie's sensitive awareness more respectfully. For Art and Barbara, the problem had gone on a lot longer than a couple of years; during the session we discovered that they had been replaying essentially the same dialogue for the entire 32 years of their relationship.

During the session, they broke through "everything's fine" to a new level of authentic communication. We facilitated them through the steps of the Ten-Minute Heart Talk (you'll find the instructions later in the book) and the process opened a floodgate of pent-up emotion for both of them.

Underneath Art's "everything's fine" were several things that weren't as good as he was leading himself to believe. Indeed, he would later say they were killing him. Basically, he hated just about everything in his life: he hated his job, he hated his car, he hated the house they lived in, he hated that he was 40 pounds overweight and had a gym membership he never used. He listed a dozen or so other things he didn't like about his life.

Barbara listened to Art's impassioned rant with her jaw slack: "Why don't you ever *talk to me* about these things?" Talking with integrity sounds your unique tone freely, allowing your partner or close friends to deeply feel your essence and what you're discovering about yourself as you talk. Communication isn't about who did what and who's in control. It's about expressing who you are and who you are becoming, and is one of the greatest treasures of mature relating.

The Deepest Integrity

Beyond the kind of integrity that makes life work well lies a deeper integrity that goes to the very center of ourselves. It is the very question of who we are and who we are becoming—whether we are in harmony with our true purpose in life. At some point at midlife or beyond, each of us needs to face ourselves unflinchingly and ask:

Am I doing what I most want to do during my precious time on earth?

Am I cultivating my unique genius?

Am I expressing my genius successfully, by my own chosen standards, in the world?

These are questions that conscious couples must confront, because not to do so is to invite an erosion of intimacy at the very center of the relationship. From Chapter One you know the positive impact on your relationships of liberating your own creativity. You also know the increasingly negative impact of denying a voice to your creativity at midlife and later.

The reason the issue of creativity becomes magnified as you proceed into your 50s and into your full maturity is this: creativity is an integrity issue. Your creative potential is a fundamental force, like gravity, that needs to be honored at all times and exerts more and more of a pull as you mature. To be out of integrity with your creativity—particularly that aspect of your creativity we call your *genius*—is to be in disharmony down deep where it matters most inside you.

Like your thumbprint, your unique creative genius is completely your own. Your genius may come to light in many different places. Your genius may just as easily be called forth composing a world-class soup as composing a timeless symphony. In other words, your genius is usually the way you pay attention to something, not the "something" itself.

To discover and express your own singular creativity is, at a very deep level, what the journey of life is all about. It's all too easy in modern life to get sidetracked into paths that distract you from discovering your genius. You can be the most prosperous stockbroker or attorney in town, but if your creative genius isn't being engaged in your work, it's a setup for rampant dissatisfaction. Being out of integrity with your genius causes a wobble that destabilizes your relationships and your health as well as your work.

We've been there, both in our own lives and in working with many people facing the same issues. Gay was once so out of integrity with his genius that he was living an entire life at odds with it. As he explains:

> At 24 I was grossly obese, weighed 320 pounds—140 pounds more than the 180 I weighed this morning. I also smoked two to three packs of cigarettes a day and was in a relationship where loud, daily conflict was the norm. I also hated my job and the part of the world I lived in. I'd moved from Florida, where I spent the first 22 years of my life hating the heat and bugs, to Northern New England, which had a winter my Floridian mind had never contemplated. Never having seen a snowflake in my life, I was thrilled when it snowed on Labor Day. However, the romance had definitely worn off by the time it snowed on Memorial Day too.

When we're out of integrity, we usually get the gift of a wake-up call, although we may not appreciate the gift at the time. In Gay's case the wake-up call was a literal whack on the head, a slip on the ice that landed him on his back on the hardpan of a New England country road:

Although the fall didn't knock me out, I lay on the road for several minutes gathering my wits. There was a jagged rock to the right of my head, and I remember thinking, "I could be dead right now. And I would have never really lived." In that moment on the ice I realized I was not living my own life.

My father died at 32, grossly obese, a heavy smoker, in a painful relationship with my mother, who didn't know she was pregnant with me until after my father's death. There I was on the same path, out of some sort of karma or genetics that I didn't comprehend, bent on some life purpose that wasn't my own chosen one. Lying there on the ice I made a choice: to find out who I really was. Before I got up and lumbered back home, I made a commitment to do everything I could to find out how I wanted *my* life to go.

Within a year I lost a hundred pounds. In the next couple of years I would quit smoking, get myself extricated from the painful relationship, quit the job I hated, and move to Northern California, where in spite of what Mark Twain said about San Francisco weather, at least the snowflakes were few and far between.

Sometimes we hear people say they want to find out "what I came here to do." We like the general idea, but aren't fond of that phrase. For many people it implies reincarnation, which they don't believe in, so the wording puts them off. However, to get the power of the concept, you don't need to believe in reincarnation or any other religious idea. All you really need to do is change the phrase. To invoke the power of your inner genius, ask this simpler question: *What do I most love to do?*

That's what frees your creative genie from the bottle.

For example, ever since Katie could stand up she has loved to dance. Her mom, Polly, made the first entry in Katie's baby book: "She loves to pull herself up in her crib and dance!" While her love of dance brought her great joy, it also brought pain, especially in adolescence when she found that the strong, curvaceous body she'd inherited didn't resemble the stick-thin ballerina body of that time.

Fortunately, though, through one of the inspired coincidences that often take our life journeys in unimagined new directions,

Katie passed by the gymnasium one day when she was a college student, noticed unusual activity, and went in to investigate. Inside was a group of women moving across the gym saying "No!" in different ways. The women were shouting, gesturing, and stamping, all accompanied by myriad and full-body expressions of "No!" What Katie was witnessing was a class by a pioneering figure in the new field of dance therapy, Joan Smallwood. Katie was transfixed, and a career was born. She became a founding member of dance therapy's governing body and 50 years later contributes actively to the field.

In Katie's case, the baby who loved to dance found her ultimate genius as a therapist who uses movement in the healing process. As we explored the origins of genius, both in ourselves and in our clients, we made the surprising discovery that childhood play often contains the glimmer of what will become a life-defining skill in later life. For example, one of the family stories told about Gay comes courtesy of his mom, Norma Hendricks, a newspaper columnist who wrote lots of funny stuff about him when he was a kid (stuff that he would, of course, later find terribly embarrassing as an adolescent). "When I was four years old," he says, "Mom noted that I liked to listen to family stories, then make up happier endings for them. That same year I also made an office out of a cardboard box and installed it in the corner of my grandparents' living room. I told family members they were welcome to come and discuss their problems with me. I don't recall that any of them ever took me up on the offer, probably because I wore short pants and commuted to the office on a tricycle."

Take a moment to reflect on your own version of our stories. Can you see the early origins of your genius in the kinds of play you most loved to do as a child? Gay says, "I've always found it fascinating that Mom noticed the budding moments of an activity I would later spend thousands of hours of my adult life doing. As a therapist and seminar leader for forty-five years, I've helped many people make up better endings to family stories they inherited. As a novelist and screenwriter, I've also spent thousands of hours making up stories I hope are as interesting as the family tales I heard growing up." (However, the real stories of the Hendricks, Garrett, and Carroll clans—ranging from plantation owners to hardscrabble farmers, from riverboat gamblers and deep-woods bourbon alchemists to philanthropists and authors—are so incredible that Gay would never try to outdo them in fiction. He's saving his family stories for a memoir to amuse himself with if he ever gets around to retiring.)

Everything You Know Is Wrong

We wish we'd had classes on integrity and relationships in our elementary school years, right alongside other basics such as grammar, subtraction, and the names of the state capitals. We didn't, though, and you probably didn't either. Indeed, some instruction in high school or college on the same subject would have been appreciated. We didn't get it there either, so, probably like you, we had to learn about integrity in the rough-and-tumble world of raw experience, otherwise known as "making a lot of mistakes."

There are a couple of big places where people mess up most in relationship. These are places where integrity matters the most in keeping the daily flow of intimacy going. The first one is integrity of feeling. Are we covering up important feelings under a glaze of "I'm fine's"? Are we stuffing the joy, sorrow, fear, and anger we authentically feel? Are we sharing all our feelings with our beloveds? The first level of integrity is whether we are being true to ourselves.

The second level is integrity in speaking, when what you're saying out loud fits with what you know to be true inside you. The moment you speak something true, whether it's "I'm angry right now" or "I stole your money," it produces a unique feeling of alignment inside you. We once asked a seasoned detective what he had learned in his career that most surprised him. Without hesitation he said, "How good people feel when they confess." He told us he got cards every Christmas from people in prison, thanking him for helping them get into integrity. Even though their confessions to him had landed them in prison, they had also experienced that feeling of alignment in his presence.

Focus for a moment on the physics of integrity rather than the morality of it. If you turn the water in a garden hose on full blast and then screw down the nozzle tight so that the water can't get out, pressure builds up in the hose as the forces of flow meet the resistance of the nozzle. That's essentially the situation when we go out of integrity in speaking truth. In us humans as well as the hose, eventually something has to give. In the hose, leaks start to fizz and bubble around the seal. In humans, we make a slip of the tongue that reveals the hidden truth, or we get outright busted, supposedly hiking the Appalachian Trail on a solo vision quest when we're actually romancing our beloved in Buenos Aires, as infamously happened to the former governor of South Carolina.

However the nozzle gets opened, whether it's through a conscious revealing of the truth or a coerced confession, there's usually a rush as the pent-up flow is liberated. Then the flow refines itself and becomes steady. That's why we say that integrity is a matter of physics as much as of morality. We've been privileged to witness, on hundreds of occasions, the miracle that happens when the nozzle opens and the flow is restored.

The third level of integrity comes from harmony of action, when your choices align with your values and authentic experience. One of the hardest things for a human being to admit is "What I'm doing isn't working." It's a human habit, handed down from ancient times, to assume that if we just did the same thing we're doing but made it bigger, louder, faster, or better, we'd eventually solve the problem. This is the type of thinking that has us raise our voices in an attempt to communicate with a person who doesn't speak our language.

Unfortunately, it sometimes takes literally hundreds of run-throughs of the same conflict before a couple finally admits what's been so obvious to everyone else: what we're doing isn't working. Clients of ours who are recovering alcoholics have often told us of the relief they felt when they finally made the admission that their lives were out of control due to their drinking. Family and friends had been giving them the same message, sometimes for decades and often loudly, but it wasn't until the addict admitted it deep inside that change began to happen.

There's a comedy album by the legendary troupe The Firesign Theatre called *Everything You Know Is Wrong*. Eventually, we came to that point of humble admission in our own relationship. It wasn't easy; both of us have been compared unfavorably to mules in regard to our stubbornness.

Katie's stubbornness is legendary in her family. She attended her first day of school and gave it a full morning of her attention before slipping off unnoticed and walking a mile back home. Her mother, surprised by Katie's early return, and more than surprised that she had found her way home by herself, asked her what was wrong. Katie said, "I just don't think school is for me." Pressed for more detail, she got down to the crunch of it. "None of those kids know how to read yet. I thought school was for learning new things, so I left."

After a panicked call from the school and a gentle lecture from Mom on the workings of the world, Katie reluctantly returned to the fold and squirmed through another few years. Fortunately a gifted teacher, Mrs. Morgan, lured the lifelong kinesthetic learner out of her and helped her become an A student.

Gay came by his stubbornness partly by inheritance:

My mother was the most stubborn person I've ever known in my life, except for my grandmother. My grandmother was so stubborn that, after backing her car into somebody's bumper somewhere around 1950, she refused thereafter to drive her car in reverse. If she got into a situation that required her to back up, she would go into a store and call somebody. I know, because once I got my learner's permit at 14, I was the one who got dispatched to do her reversing for her.

I grew up in the South, in a setting right out of a William Faulkner novel, surrounded by aunts, uncles, and grandparents who lived in separate houses on the same extended piece of property. My aunt Lyndelle lived up the street and often dropped by our house in the evening on her way over to visit my grandparents around the corner from us. At the time of the evening she'd visit, Lyndelle would usually be a tumbler or so into the quart of vodka she strictly rationed herself to every night. My mother, a righteous teetotaler, disapproved mightily of my aunt's drinking. However, Mom lacked the moral leverage to get my aunt or anybody in the family to stop their bad habits, possibly because she smoked a pack of unfiltered Camel cigarettes every day and usually had a cup of coffee in her hand.

My mother and I were in the midst of some argument when my aunt popped in—nobody would have ever thought of knocking. Mom summed up what was happening by telling my aunt about my awesome stubbornness. My aunt endeared herself to me for all time by appraising my mother up and down in slow motion and saying, "Where could he have ever gotten a thing like that?" I can still remember my mother's jaw-dropped expression, so expecting sisterly support and then so outraged at my aunt's comment that she refused to speak to her for several months.

You can probably see why it was so hard for us to realize that everything we knew was wrong. Once we took that big gulp and admitted we needed to drop everything we knew and start from scratch, our relationship took off on a benign rocket ride that we're still experiencing to this day. In fact, we experience it more every day. That's what we want for you too.

Whether you're in a committed relationship now or in the process of clearing your space to welcome a new one, you enter a new dimension of possibility the moment you get sincere and humble enough to let go of everything you think you know about relationships and start from scratch. It takes awesome courage for two people to look each other in the eye and say, "What we're doing isn't working. If we really love each other, let's try something brand new."

Later in the chapter we'll go inside such a moment with a couple we'll call Barry and Saul. By noticing the steps it took for them to start from scratch and establish integrity in their relationship, you'll see how you can make powerful new commitments that produce long-lasting results—and stick with the changes so that the past doesn't overtake you again. You'll also see more evidence that integrity might just be the long-awaited all-purpose aphrodisiac, the one that works all the time and won't cause you to flunk a drug test or Breathalyzer.

Integrity in Sexuality

What Barry and Saul will confront, and what just about all of us confront eventually, is that sexual integrity is at the heart of many of our other problems with integrity. What is sexual integrity? It's simple. Full sexual integrity is when you:

1. Celebrate all your sexual feelings
2. Express your sexual feelings only in ways that honor your own well-being and the promises you've made

Right away you can probably see why we humans struggle so much around integrity in sex. Once, in front of a congenial audience, we said, "Raise your hand if you've ever hidden your sexual feelings, perhaps even from yourself." About two-thirds of the hands went up. Then we said, "Keep them raised or raise them if you've ever had sex in a way that dishonored yourself or broke promises you'd made to someone else." Pretty much every hand in the place was up, as ours were too.

It takes most of us some time to learn how to celebrate all our sexual feelings. It also takes a lot of learning—usually the painful trial-and-error kind—to figure out how to express those sexual feelings only in ways that honor our beloveds and the promises we've made, including the ones we've made to ourselves.

Integrity matters so much in sexual relationships for one big, simple reason: we all got here through sex and relationships. From the moment the head of the sperm cell erupts and releases its cargo into the egg, we're all everlastingly enmeshed in a matrix of relationships. Any situation that involves events such as being invaded by a foreign body, having your head explode, having your individuality annihilated, two things becoming one then immediately starting to divide into parts—well, let's just say it's fertile ground for relationship drama later on.

Explore the beginnings of your relationship history for a moment. For example, what was the quality of your egg and sperm donors' relationship the day or night you were conceived? Many people have told us family stories that one or both of their parents were drunk at their conception. Others have told us that their conception was a last-ditch attempt to save a deteriorating relationship, one that ultimately failed despite the attempt to rescue it by having a baby. Or perhaps you got the fairy-tale version— you were wanted, loved, and cared for by people who really wanted to be there. Whether you got the fairy tale or one of the more complicated versions, you're just like the rest of us in one important respect: you got here through thousands of generations of sexy ancestors. The sooner we admit it, the faster we can grow in relationships.

We've been helping people sort out sexual dramas through four decades now, a period in history in which sexual behavior has changed radically. Throughout all those changes in the way people think about sex, integrity has remained as the fundamental issue. For example, we've counseled young people who were afraid that their sexual attractions to people of the same gender made them inferior in the eyes of God. We'll tell you a particularly poignant story about one of them later.

At the other end of the spectrum, we've also counseled the adult victims of sexual abuse by a philandering guru who cleaned out the ashram's money and skipped town. Even in the extremes of those two situations, it's not sex that's the problem: the real problem is being lied to about sex and lying to others about sex.

In the case of the guru, think of how much suffering could have been avoided if he had stood up in front of his followers and told the truth. Maybe it would have been in the same meeting room at the ashram where we would later sit in a circle to work with a hundred or so survivors of the travesty of spirituality his lies had landed them in.

Knowing what we know now about the circumstances, we imagine he might have said something like this:

I'm standing in front of you rather than seated on the throne you always see me on because I want to speak to you as an equal. I have a problem I don't know what to do with. Because you always see my wife and me smiling together in public, you may not know that I have been miserable in my marriage for many years. As you probably do know, it is an arranged marriage with a woman I adore, but with whom I was matched when I was in junior high school. We've never been attracted to each other physically, but our strong sense of duty made us want to please our parents so much that we eventually married. Even having our children was a long struggle about which we still bicker constantly in private. From before we were married I have felt sexual attraction to many women and have had sex with more than ten women without my wife's knowledge. Several of those ten women are here in this room. I have spoken to them in private to receive their permission to speak to you like this, and before doing so I made a full and frank admission to my wife. I was shocked to discover that my indiscretions were anything but a surprise to her. Indeed, I was humiliated to discover that my behavior, which I thought so discreet, was the subject of gossip.

As you know, I was raised in a very spiritual household in India. The most revered members of my extended family were celibate monks and priests, those who transcended their base sexual desires to live in the full practice of the spiritual life. That all sounded wonderful until one day when I was 13 years old. I felt the awakening of sexual feelings in me. At the same time I felt the hot shame of spiritual impurity all over me. From that moment on I've never known what to do with my sexual feelings. Now it's brought me here, to confess that I have abused the very power your hearts freely gave me. I'm beginning to feel a flicker of compassion for the person I obviously am, the flawed person to whom you've given your devotion, but I feel utmost compassion for you.

I have it easy. I will resign today and attempt to listen to each and every person whom I've wounded through my acts of unconsciousness. I will focus on righting the integrity here in this community until it has been restored, whether or not you ever want to see me again.

You, though, will have a task so awesome I'm not sure I, your former teacher, would have the courage to do it. After you have exhausted your rage, your grief, and all the other feelings about me to which

43

you are absolutely entitled by my acts of unconsciousness, you will deal with the monster at the mouth of the cave: what made you hand over your spiritual well-being and your money to another human being in the first place? I'm confronting that monster every day myself right now, and I can tell you it sure isn't fun. My version of it goes like this: what made me create a community of thousands of people who adore me and gave me millions of dollars, then lie to them and con them into thinking I was something I wasn't? The only thing I can think of that would make me do such a vile thing is that I have tried to hate and silence my sexual feelings all my life and I can no longer do so. I want to celebrate my sexual feelings and welcome them into the full spiritual being that's the real me. But I often feel such loathing for myself and my sexuality that I still feel that same kind of hot shame as when my mother caught me masturbating when I was a youngster.

Now to the particulars. I'll stay here today as long as I'm welcome, and I commit to listening to anything you have to say or telling you anything you want to know until I topple over asleep or we all agree to go rest. Then I'm available however and whenever you want to connect, until the day I die.

The guru didn't say any of that, though. Instead, he cleaned out the accounts and skipped town in the middle of the night. If he had had that conversation, it would have made our job easier when we sat down with the survivors some months after the guru's midnight flight. As it was, it took three complicated days. That experience was worthy of a book or two on its own, but the essentials were the same in a much simpler conversation we had with a young woman who was trying to sort out her complicated feelings about her sexuality.

Diana, a woman in her late 40s, approached us after a talk we gave in the Midwest. She waited until we'd been signing books for half an hour or so, then came forward as we were packing our things to go. "May I ask you a question?" she said with a shy smile. "I have come all the way from Albania to ask it of you."

That's something you don't hear every day. We put down our things and gave her our full attention. It turned out to be a priceless moment in our lives.

Diana's journey to us had started in Albania 20 years before when, as a nun, she read a German translation of one of our books. Now no longer a nun and working in a sausage factory outside Chicago, she had seen an announcement that we were coming to town and had taken the bus over to hear our talk. We noticed she was clutching a stack of several of our books, all well thumbed and full of yellow stickers on pages. We signed her books and waited to hear the question she'd come from Albania to ask.

She got right to the point: "I need to know—are the feelings I have for my friend sick and evil?" Then she said, "My friend is a woman."

Without even hearing her story we could feel in our hearts the years of struggle, misinformation, and shaming it took to make her ask that question. We were moved by her resilience and courage. She was gazing at Gay with rapt attention, as if she needed to hear the information from a father figure. As best we can recollect it, here's how the conversation went.

Gay said to Diana, "When I tune in to you and your feelings, I don't feel anything at all sick or evil. Don't take my word for it, though. Right now, just feel those feelings you have for your friend for a moment." She nodded, a smile at the corners of her mouth. Gay asked her how they felt, and she said, "Only beautiful."

Katie told her, "Your feelings *are* beautiful. The only question now is whether you will choose to celebrate and tell the truth about your feelings, or lie about them to others."

Diana visibly shuddered. "My relatives . . ." she said, trailing off in a tone of voice you didn't have to be Albanian to interpret. Tears forming at the corners of her eyes, she said, "I may have to choose between them and the love I feel."

Katie gave her a gentle reminder: "No, all you have to do is choose between telling the truth or lying about the love you feel. Each way has consequences, but if you choose to tell the truth, *your relatives* will choose whether to accept or reject the real you. Telling the truth will not be what drives them away. Your truth gives them the opportunity to love the real you, and if they can't do that, *they* will then choose to reject the real you. It's their right, and it's really none of your business which one they choose. Your business is honoring your feelings and being honest about them."

Diana thanked us and gave us each a hug, gathered her armload of books, and went off to pursue her destiny. We've never seen her since in person, but we occasionally hear from her when she and her partner celebrate some milestone such as buying their first house.

What does a conversation about sex with an Albanian lesbian have in common with the shenanigans of a 60-year-old guru? The answer: although they grew up in cultures as different as you can imagine—Diana the tenth child of a poor family in Albania, the guru the treasured only son of a Brahmin family in India—we can imagine both of them experiencing the integrity wobble inside and out because of being lied to about their sexuality. Long before they could think for themselves, both Diana and the guru had been tragically misinformed about the very nature of reality. They were taught that we must stand in constant judgment of our feelings, labeling some of them "good" and some of them "bad." This is supposed to make the good ones stick around and the bad ones go away. Many of us humans are taught this lesson. When religion enters the picture, the message is ratcheted up a few notches: now we're told that our good feelings come from God and the bad ones from the Devil.

After a while those judgments solidify and pile up like boulders in a river. The boulders don't dam up the river completely, but all those piles of judgment create barriers in the flow of wholeness. The barriers keep us from fully savoring our richest emotions; they also keep us from creating relationships that are safe spaces for the celebration of those emotions.

In both Diana and the guru, a powerful judge had been installed on the banks of the river, constantly trying to figure out which part of the water was bad, wrong, or sinful. In Diana's situation, her inner judge was presiding over a potential criminal trial: when she was growing up in Albania, homosexuality was a crime. In the guru's world, culturally inserted inner judges regularly inspected the river for signs of spiritual impurity and found a great amount of it.

In other words, both of them suffered from a thinking error deliberately installed in them by culture and religion. The error: thinking that if we label some of our inner experience "good" and some "bad," the good stuff will stay and the bad stuff will go away. The thinking error arises from assuming that simply using different labels can contradict and disrupt authentic internal experiences. Labeling usually adds another layer of debris that eventually needs to be cleared up for wholeness to be restored.

They also suffered from a second thinking error, also very likely installed early in life by people who were themselves suffering in anguish and shame over some aspect of their sexuality. The error: *If I can keep the truth hidden about my integrity violations, it will be just like they never happened!* Most of us have figured out the flaw in that particular line of logic by the time we exit junior high school—usually through being busted doing all the things kids do. However, many high-profile politicians do not seem to get this bit of essential wisdom until they are well along the Appalachian Trail of life.

Unshaming Sex

About 15 percent of the couples we've worked with are in same-sex relationships; about 20 percent of the singles who come to our seminars and offices are seeking a same-sex relationship. Since 1980, the year we started working together, there's been such a huge change in attitude toward gay people and relationships that it would be hard to believe had we not witnessed it. Think, though, of how much individual and collective suffering occurred to bring those changes about. How much of that suffering could have been avoided if generations of gay people hadn't been lied to and shamed about their sexuality?

Saul and Barry had been together for five years before the laws changed in their state. They'd stood in a long line to get married that very day, and all had gone well for the next six months. Suddenly one day, in Saul's words, "Barry turned into my father." According to Saul, Barry became increasingly controlling, manipulative, cold, and condescending. That wasn't exactly how Barry saw it, though. According to him, the problem was Saul. If Saul hadn't gotten so damn stingy with sex all of a sudden, everything would be fine. Predictably, this point of view caused Saul to go wild with frustration. "Barry says that *every* time we try to talk about this."

Their story is a good example of what many couples go through in relationships. Two people have what looks like two completely different issues on the surface, but without knowing it they are both actually struggling with the same and far deeper issue.

A famous scene in the movie *Annie Hall* came to mind when Barry and Saul told us why they had come for counseling. In the movie, the Diane Keaton character and the Woody Allen character are talking to their respective therapists. On a split screen we get to see how each one answers a question about how often they have sex. Keaton says, with exasperation, "Constantly. Probably three times a week," while Allen is saying to his therapist, "Hardly ever. Probably three times a week."

In Saul's view, Barry focused on sex far too much. Barry didn't see it that way, though. In Barry's view, Saul had always been stingy with sex. This drama had been playing out for most of the now seven years they'd been together. They met in the context of San Francisco's club scene; the first year of their relationship involved a lot of partying. But then Saul, 55, wanted to settle down, buy a house, perhaps adopt a child. Saul said, "Frankly, I don't care if I ever stay up dancing 'til two A.M. again in my life." Barry, a few years younger than Saul, still liked to hit the clubs at least once a week.

The drama played out in several ways, including a long-drawn-out compromise that never settled the issue: Saul occasionally and reluctantly went out clubbing with Barry, while Barry reluctantly stayed home almost every night. Although compromise is widely touted as a solution in relationships, it only works if the compromise doesn't make everybody too miserable. This one grated on them for years, but they could never find anything to do about it except recycle the same tired arguments over and over. They had been stewing in this issue for pretty much the whole length of their time together. We wanted to help them snap out of the trance of negativity long enough to open up new positive possibilities.

One of the fastest ways we've ever discovered to start a process of rapid relationship transformation is to change one specific word. We've seen this word-swap work its magic on many occasions, and it did so with Barry and Saul.

They'd been expressing their anger to each other, in ways both loud and subtle, for years without the problem ever changing. It was very easy for them to say to each other, "I'm angry about _____" and fill in the blank with a litany of peeves.

This time, they changed "I'm angry" to "I'm scared."

One thing we learned early in our own relationship was that anytime we were angry we were also scared and sad. Fear and sadness are two other feelings that must be acknowledged if any anger issue is to be resolved permanently. Even when you've been stuck in the trance of anger as long as Barry and Saul, you only need a few moments outside the trance to break free of it. It's like the moment when you wake up from a bad dream—you didn't know you were dreaming until you snapped out of it.

Barry and Saul were quivering with anger when Katie gently said, "Now tune in to what you're afraid of and sad about underneath all that anger. Feel what's going on in your hearts and your bellies."

They looked at us blankly, as in "What are you talking about?" They had come to the end of their map; we were asking them to jump off into unknown territory. Fortunately they were courageous enough to take the big leap. We asked them to stand up, so they could have their feet firmly on the ground, and to face each other a couple of feet apart.

"Look into each other's eyes and take an easy breath or two. Then, say something simple like 'I'm scared that . . .' or 'I'm sad about . . .'"

Instantly they let go of the bristling attitude and dropped into a state of benign confusion. We call it a "benign" form of confusion because it leads to wonder, new alignment between inner experience and expression, and ultimate resolution.

"I don't get it," Barry said.

"Me neither," Saul said.

Katie made the invitation a new way. "Notice where in your body you feel scared. Just point to it."

Barry pointed to his belly.

"Mine's up here," Saul said, clutching his hand to his neck.

"And then point to any places where you feel sad," Katie said.

Confusion reigned again briefly, and then they both pointed in the general direction of their chests.

Gay said, "So the message here is, underneath your anger at each other are equally important deeper feelings. The main ones that need your attention are sadness and fear. If you don't talk about those, you just keep recycling the anger on the surface."

They got it. Katie said, "Be with yourself for a moment, scanning your body with your awareness. See if you can put your finger on one specific thing you're scared about."

Barry said, "I'm scared I'm never going to please you."

Saul said, "I'm scared you're going to leave me for somebody younger."

We discussed those feelings with them for a few moments and then asked a question that often inspires another major shift in consciousness: "Barry, when you tune in to that sense of never being able to please Saul, does it feel familiar to you?"

"What do you mean by 'familiar'?" he asked, back in benign confusion again.

"Like you've experienced it in other situations before you met Saul."

"Ah," he said, rocking back on his heels, a faraway look in his eyes. We noticed Saul was holding his breath.

"Everybody breathe," Gay said, taking a big in-breath and letting it go with an audible "Aahh."

It turned out that Saul was but the latest in a long line of men Barry hadn't been able to please, starting with his father. Indeed, we discovered that Barry had never experienced an honest, face-to-face conversation about his sexuality with his father, now dead for many years.

When we're confronted with something unacceptable to our brain in its current configuration—like a son's sexual orientation—a quick way to bring peace again to our roiling synapses is to seal out the invading concept and take cover behind a wall of judgment. Once we seal the concept out, we have to come up with a label for it, the reason we're shutting it out. The five most popular labels are:

It's wrong.
It's bad.
It's sick.
It's stupid.
It's crazy.

With regard to Barry's sexuality, his father was a solid five-for-five. Barry told us that even into his father's declining years he still occasionally sent Barry clippings from fundamentalist publications, articles about LGBT people who had joyously returned to heterosexuality after straying into the sinful lifestyle choices of the gay world. As Barry put it, his father was "Old School before they invented Old School."

Barry's parents had split up when he was five. His older brother had gone to live with Dad, while Barry stayed with Mom. Barry remembered his parents arguing about him—his tone of voice, his way of walking, and the things he liked to play with—so different from his star-athlete older brother. In essence, from the time Barry could walk and talk he had been the subject of criticism by his father. As we heard more of his story, though, a deeper layer of rejection came forth. It turned out that Barry's very existence had been the subject of argument and criticism even before he was conceived. His father was happy with one son and didn't want any more children. His mother very much wanted more kids and got pregnant "by accident" against her husband's wishes.

In other words, his father's negative feelings about Barry got there before Barry did. Barry's very existence was a criticism waiting to happen. Is it any surprise that he would unconsciously select a series of relationships in which he felt criticized constantly?

Then, into his life came Saul—fit, older, and athletic like Barry's big brother. It was a perfect setup for both of them, in the sense that they were ripe for projecting onto each other. Saul hadn't realized it yet, but he had a theme in his relationships too: one that interlocked so perfectly (and often maddeningly) with Barry's pattern that it looked as if they'd been set up for maximum drama by Central Casting. Even Saul's job played a role in the drama: he spent all day every day consulting with hotels and restaurants about ways to tighten up their kitchen procedures. In other words, from 9 to 5 he was always looking for things that didn't work, things to fix that would make complex human endeavors more efficient. It was hard for him to turn off his looking-for-what's-wrong skill when he came home. Trouble usually followed, because Barry didn't appreciate being looked at like a complex human endeavor that needed to be fixed for efficiency's sake.

"I'm scared" turned the drama around. When they stopped recycling what they were angry about and started talking about what they were scared and sad about, the energy in the room changed dramatically. Now they were two people, both scared and confused, rather than two angry enemies.

Katie asked, "Are you willing to be allies in moving through to a good resolution?" She got agreement from both of them. That by itself was a huge accomplishment for Saul and Barry. It's a big undertaking for an efficiency consultant to stop looking for what's wrong, just as big as asking a person who's been criticized all his life to conceive of a life free of criticism. Commitment is where you have to begin with any major process of life change, though; it's essential to have both people plant their feet on the ground and say, "Yes, this is what we commit to."

It's a heroic move. When you both commit, you take a stand in the present that renders the past irrelevant. Making a new commitment to be allies is a powerful step to release the grip of the old pattern of interacting as enemies and to return to the wholeness that integrity moves generate.

With the commitment to work as allies, they were ready to explore the big new area of the unknown. Gay opened up that territory by asking, "Can you conceive of a relationship free of criticism and blame?" Their blank stares and stunned silence answered the question.

It's like asking a fish to conceive of taking a stroll on dry land. At some long-ago point in our own ancestral history, some of our distant relatives, fishlike beings with good imaginations, not only dreamed up a life on dry land but also managed to get up on it and stagger around long enough to get their evolutionary footing. Of course, it took 50 million years or so to pull off this magic move. Now, standing successfully atop all that trial-and-error learning, we tend to take for granted what was actually an amazing and unique feat. Strutting about proudly on our back limbs, we have trouble conceiving of what our lives were like back when we lived in the water. As hard as it is for us to imagine human life before we were land creatures, it's often even harder to imagine a life free of a pattern we've been stuck in.

That's why Barry and Saul had those stunned looks on their faces. They literally could not conceive of a life beyond criticism.

Finally Barry asked, "What would that look like?"

That question opened the door to the future of their relationship, and over the next few weeks we assisted them in building a completely new kind of communication between them.

For the details of how they did it, and how you can do it, take a deep breath and dedicate yourself to some intense learning about one of the most important issues you'll ever encounter.

CHAPTER THREE

Full-Spectrum
Presencing

There's no single word that expresses the act of being present, so 20 years ago we decided to make up a new one: *presencing*. When we type *presencing* on our computer, it always comes up with a red line under it, meaning that Microsoft Word considers it nonexistent. Someday, though, we predict it will stop turning red, because it's one of the most important keys to transforming relationships at midlife.

Here's our simple definition of presencing: the act of consciously focusing attention on what is happening in the present moment. Presencing is the opposite of what goes on much of the time in relationships: our bodies are there but our hearts and minds are someplace else. Presencing brings everything back together and puts the full resources of your consciousness to work on increasing the flow of love in your life. Presencing provides the juice for creative flow and gives practical life to your integrity commitments.

Presencing becomes increasingly important in relationships at midlife and beyond. After midlife, there is more and more past to get lost in, and less and less future to cast your aspirations into. The present is the only moment when the miracle of transformation can take place, and fortunately even a small amount of presencing can set those miracles in action.

Full-Spectrum Presencing is an integrative body-mind tool that helps you welcome feelings, sensations, thoughts, and any other experience into the wholeness of yourself and expand your direct experience of integrity. One of the big challenges in relationships is that when something feels missing in our inner wholeness, we often unconsciously try to find it in a partner. In other words, if we don't like who we are, we often try to confirm that we're lovable by demanding that our partners prove their love. That never works, though, because genuine self-esteem is an inside job that comes to life through presencing-filled integrity.

What's It All About Anyway?

The Monty Python troupe posed that question brilliantly in their movie *The Meaning of Life,* but humans have been asking it in one form or another for millennia. To set your priorities at midlife and later requires the ability to be still for a few moments in the space of a big question such as "What do I most want to experience and accomplish during my time here?" Questions of that magnitude often make people squirm; some people squirm out of answering them their whole lives. To get beneath the squirm requires cultivation of the skill of Full-Spectrum Presencing.

Ultimately, what counts in the irreplaceable moments of your life is a question more fundamental even than your life purpose: was I actually present? You have the same challenge all of us face, whether or not you are here for every moment of life. Here and now is the only place where you can connect with yourself or other people. If you're standing at the altar saying "I do" with your mouth while your mind is checking out someone in the front row, your "I do" will have something missing from it. What's missing in many of the important moments of life is the sense of being fully present.

All our courtship rituals and all our efforts to understand love are designed to make a certain dream come true—the experience of being completely real and open as we resonate in harmony with another person who is also being real and open. It's the skill of presencing that brings those dreams to life. In order to feel the flow of intimacy all the time in our lives, we first have to cultivate the ability to be present for it a few seconds at a time. It's a challenge for most of us at first to rest in the stillness and vibrance of our essential selves while we're in harmony with another person. Such a challenge, in fact, that it inspired the late Eric Berne, M.D., founder of Transactional Analysis, to say that most people don't experience 15 minutes of genuine intimacy in their lifetimes. You're not "most people," though; if you're reading this book, you're very likely the kind of person who thinks, *Well, if most people don't experience fifteen minutes of intimacy, I'm going to do everything I possibly can to experience it every minute.*

In our experience there are awesome rewards to dedicating yourself to living in the present. You get an immediate reward, because you experience longer periods of presence before drifting or getting distracted. In life, you get what you focus on, so take a moment right now to commit yourself, body and soul, to learning how to be present for all the moments of your life. Affirm this in your mind: "I'm keenly interested in learning how to be present all the time. I dedicate myself consciously to learning everything I can about it."

The bigger reward comes down the line, after you've applied yourself for a while to increasing the amount of time you spend in the present. One day, as you are being present with one feeling or another—simply letting yourself feel it with no agenda other than increasing your sensitive awareness—you make a stunning realization. You see that you've been in the grip of a popular human delusion: that there is one faucet marked "Pleasure" and another marked "Pain." You've been trying to keep the first one wide open and the other one turned off. Suddenly you realize there is only one faucet; you see that pain, bliss, and all other feelings come out of that same faucet. The label on the faucet is "Awareness." Once you have that awareness, the only question is how much you want to open the faucet.

It took us years to learn how to keep the faucet open all the time, to feel the flow of intimacy, of loving closeness within ourselves and with each other, in every moment every day. It probably won't take you as long, because you have a map we didn't have in the early stages of our journey. We had to draw the map along the way, which required making large numbers of mistakes and figuring out how to fix them. You also have a new understanding of presencing: the magic that can happen when you turn presence into a verb.

Instead of waiting for moments when you and your partner are free to connect, you actively bring your Full-Spectrum Present self with you, all the time, wherever you are. Your presencing opens a space for your partner's whole self to bloom. Your mutual presencing welcomes discovery and a felt sense of oceanic depth that you can continuously dive into and bring up treasures from. Presencing creates genuine magic, daily magic that turns moments of connection into bliss balls that can be tossed and ignited into fireworks or spread over your day like honey. One moment of genuine presence can erase decades of distance. Presence can replace the adrenaline addiction that fuels most relationships through the gotcha game.

In his poem "The Lovers," the Danish poet Morten Søndergaard tells of a future world in which we are all fully present in our relationships. In this new world, "orgasms need never come to an end. Roses function as currency . . . the words 'you' and 'I' are now synonymous." To live in that state of flow is the high possibility of relationships at midlife and beyond, and Full-Spectrum Presencing is the gateway.

Empty Nest or Open Field?

Presencing solves a problem that almost nothing else will solve. After midlife, couples and single parents often enter a phase that has been labeled "empty nest." We've worked with hundreds of couples and singles facing the so-called empty nest, and from that experience we stopped calling it empty nest. We now prefer to call it "open field," because if you can get past the painful aspect of children moving on, it can be a boundary-free space of infinite exploration. It can be a challenge, though, to dismantle the complex matrix of appointments, assignments, and arrangements for children's needs and the business of family life. Often, around this same time, career focus shifts or ends in its accustomed form. Partners enter a realm where their conversations and their connection become primary.

When we went through this phase ourselves, we noticed a definite shift of energy when there was nothing blocking direct connection at any time. We were used to fielding questions all day such as, "Did you remember to pay the orthodontist's bill?" and "Mom, have you seen my baseball glove?" When those conversations stopped, we suddenly had an opportunity to choose anew every day whether we wanted to live in an empty nest or an open field. We chose the open field, but it was not without some missteps and mishaps along the way. More than once we found ourselves wondering, "What are we supposed to talk about now that we're the only ones around?"

To picture the scope of this change, imagine that you and all your immediate family have been tied together by elastic bands that stretch and interweave. This connection basket has created meaning and structure for many years. Then imagine those cords being loosened one by one until just the cord connecting the two of you remains. This phase transition can be daunting for people who haven't stepped into the possibilities of presencing together.

The Power of Attention

People get into attention habits in relationship very quickly, often in the first exchanges of their meeting. These habits become invisible, crooked foundations for their own Leaning Tower of Pisa that grows askew along with the relationship. Here are some examples we've seen over the years with couples.

- People don't actually face each other fully when communicating.

- Attention skips like a pebble over a pond, never really landing either inside one partner or with the other.

- Partners are multitasking their attention, giving only a trickle to the other in the midst of tasks and lists.

- One person is constantly chasing the other's attention, while the other withholds or is just not at home: an adult version of "Look at me!"

- Couples interpret and respond to gestures or looks as if they're real without noticing that their own attention is creating the meaning.

- Partners have allowed others, such as children, to interrupt the bond of their primary attention to each other for so long that empty-nesting also means empty attention reservoir.

- "In a minute" or "when I'm done" has taken precedence over the primary commitment to give attention to your beloved.

- One person retreats back inside and won't give attention or gives attention in very stingy doses.

- One partner gets completely absorbed in the other, losing awareness of what she or he is actually experiencing and wanting.

These attention habits erode the very heart of conscious loving and the magic potential of mature relationships. The practice of presencing cleans out the grit and opens the full flow of loving attention, which is what most people want most deeply.

In other cultures, later life is honored. In our culture, many people experience signals to just move over and get out of the way. The call to "retire" can easily be interpreted as a request that we withdraw from society and make room for the next producers and innovators. Instead of retiring or settling into predictable attention habits, you could turn your relationship into your own living laboratory, a rich field where discovery and expansion continue to deepen. Creativity and co-creativity can become central to your lives now, a river of renewal that nourishes you and flows to everyone you contact. The art of presencing can tap into this wellspring and feed the field of connection, enriching your experience of value and generating contributions to your community.

What you *don't* do when present is just as important as the choices you do make. Your bringing yourself fully to this moment replaces:

- Reminiscing about the past, which is always arguable
- Controlling your or your mate's responses
- Second-guessing
- Criticizing
- Anticipating
- Arguing in your head
- Replying to what you thought you heard as if it were real
- Distracting
- Editing
- Hiding a feeling
- Judging
- You add your favorites here: _____

Most nonpresence, most absence of connection, occurs in the moments of contracting. Our bodies contract in fear as our deep reptilian brains get ready to fight or flee, freeze or faint. A bit farther on in the book, the chapter on moving from fear to flow can open your pipes again so you can draw presencing skills from the reservoir of available awareness. From fear to contraction to defending to distancing—that's the despair spiral. From fear to flow to curiosity to presence, integrity, and creativity—that's the growth spiral. As the scientist Bruce Lipton has said, your cells can either grow or defend, but they can't do both at the same time. What a great thing to know. Are you growing and flowing or defending and distancing? How can you tell? As you journey through this chapter, we'll move step by step into the world of Full-Spectrum Presencing, where your body wisdom and your willingness expand your connection and deepen your loving bond.

Would you be willing to cultivate this amazing ability so that you can experience infinity right here and right now with your beloved? Take a few breaths to open willingness and take the steps to experience presencing for yourself.

The Gateway to Presencing

The first step to Full-Spectrum Presencing is to trade in your habitual filters for curious appreciation. Even if you have a stack of tasks awaiting you, curious appreciation dissolves them and replaces that dense awareness with sensitive openness.

You can learn to shift to curiosity even in the midst of a habitual way of seeing your partnership. The filters that most people adopt in relationships creep in over time. Fixing, controlling, rebutting, anticipating, and more fill up the spaces where presence could flow. In contrast, when you choose to open to curiosity, you drop those filters like an old coat and free yourself to experience the right-now-ness of you and your mate. You can notice qualities about you both that had been invisible. New possibilities for resolving old issues float in on the fresh breeze of your awareness.

How do you get curious, especially in the middle of being convinced that you're right and your partner is wrong? It's actually impossible to get curious while you're holding on to being critical, blaming, or judging. Or even analyzing and lecturing your partner about what seems perfectly obvious to you. You need to enter the doorway through your whole-body awareness.

The quickest way we've found to unlock the door starts with finding your "hmmmm." You can do it right now. On your next out-breath, create a pleasant "hmmm" sound through the entire breath. Let the "hmmm" resonate through your sinuses and throat. Play with the pitch until you find the tone that feels pleasurable through your chest and head. This sound ignites wonder and shifts you from your critical brain to your curious brain.

Just that shift in awareness breaks up the logjam of habitual ways of interacting that block the flow in relationships. It makes space for what we call wonder questions. For example:

Hmmm, I wonder how I can appreciate your point of view right now?
Hmmm, I wonder how I can create something new in this interaction?
Hmmm, I wonder what I can value about you this moment?
Hmmm, I wonder how I can listen to what you really want?

Saying your wonder question out loud followed by two to three relaxed belly breaths expands curiosity and generates a flow of connection in which something new can occur. You can refresh yourself and your relating any time you shift into curiosity and add breath and wonder. Many of us have learned to jump right back into analyzing or to hunker in defense as soon as something new opens. The simple practice of "hmming" and breathing interrupts the ping-pong of habitual blame and defense that we assume is the only game we can play in Relationship World.

Deepening Presence

Once you've opened the door to presencing, how can you continue to cultivate the Full-Spectrum Presence that deepens intimacy and discovery reliably over time? You've been carrying the magic key all your life in the way you use your attention. As we've mentioned, humans need attention as much as air, water, and food. We require attention to thrive, and not just as infants. Healthy humans give and receive a full flow of awareness and attention throughout life, and in the years of midlife and beyond, you can make a quantum leap in its quality and depth. The attention nutrient can feed a garden that continues to bloom with discovery, play, and delight.

Start by giving your awareness to attention itself, the mysterious and elusive ability that humans have developed over millennia. Follow us into a simple practice that can interrupt old patterns and hone your sensitivity to creative possibilities. First, rest your awareness fully on you, then shift to bring your awareness fully to your beloved, your friend, or your colleague. Repeat. That's Loop of Awareness. Imagine the flow of awareness as an infinity sign that sweeps around you, then around your partner, then back to you, on and on. As you bring the curious "hmmm" we just explored to your whole body, you might notice your breath or a body sensation. As you shift your curious awareness to your partner, you might notice an expression or your partner's breath. Rather than reaching out and grabbing life with your expectations, Loop of Awareness allows you to receive and be nourished by the flow of awareness in much the same way that the land is nourished by the flow of a stream.

Deepening Presence Through Loop of Awareness

That's it. That's the practice. Sounds very simple, doesn't it? Just shift your awareness from you to your partner and back. Repeat throughout the day and throughout your life. What could be easier, right? So why aren't partners in later life walking Zen masters of attention? Read on to answer that question.

Gently shifting your attention from you to the other starts to chip away at the attention dams and thaw the barriers that can build up unconsciously over time. We've seen hundreds of moments where the whoosh of attraction and connection springs again from the simple gift of attention. Imagine this trickle becoming a stream, then a river, then an ocean of delight to bathe your partnership in nourishing awareness. You can open this flow choice by choice, moment by moment, as you "hmmm" your way into the ocean of essence-connection.

If you choose to make Loop of Awareness your basic practice, you'll be integrating the most effective tool for connecting deeply to you and to your beloved. This connection truly expands into infinity. When you shift your curious attention, you interrupt old patterns and make space for new interactions. New interactions juice up your experience of discovery and intimacy and renew your interest in each other.

Thinking Versus Presencing

So we should have shelves of textbooks and courses about cultivating these amazing tools of body intelligence—right? Not so much. Humans have seduced themselves with the whirring dance of thoughts for centuries. We give much more value to thoughts than to sensations. As the physicist David Bohm has said, "That's [a] mistake that thought makes. It produces a result, and then it says, I didn't do it . . ." What a great cosmic joke! We listen to the thoughts going through our minds and make them real; we ignore the sensations coursing through our bodies and judge them as irrational and crude. Try on this thought: people are afraid of the power of their authentic experience. If each of us opened to and listened closely to our whole-body experience, we'd be empowered, making different choices and thriving in indisputable aliveness.

Presencing shifts you from a focus on doing toward a focus on being. As you continue to deepen your dance of curious attention, you experience your cells opening to more contact inside you and with your partner. Picture two couples sitting at separate tables in a restaurant. One couple sits with chairs at slightly askew angles, bodies folded up, both staring off into the parking lot or at other tables. The other couple are tilted toward each other. They are talking, laughing, gesturing a lot. Their faces dance with color and expression. The second couple is drawing on the reservoir of presencing, the ongoing practice of Loop of Awareness. The first couple has definitely retired.

What Story Are You Creating?

Our bodies tell the story we've been creating about presencing throughout our lives. Most children's stories start with "Once upon a time . . ." Our partnering stories start with the habitual ways we shape our bodies with our mates and the way we use space. Does your physical posture create an opening for connection, or are your physical doors closed? Do you move at a pace that invites your partner to join you, or do you move at a pace that leaves your beloved always huffing to catch up with you?

No matter what relationship story you've created, you can shift your availability to yourself and each other through your practice of presencing. Think of presencing as a new sport you've taken up. Getting the setup takes up a lot of time in the beginning. With tennis or golf, for example, the way you frame your body generates continued discovery and learning or diminished possibility and frustration.

How can you create the ideal frame for presencing? Here are some simple suggestions to weave into your interactions starting now:

- Turn fully toward your partner when you are together.

- Open your posture so that your arms and legs are uncrossed and your body is comfortably expanded.

- Breathe easily into your belly.

Here's how each of these moves contributes to presencing.

People often underestimate the power of turning toward another while communicating. When you open your posture and face your partner, you create the widest frame for resonance and mutual sparking. When you half turn or multitask, you aren't really present anywhere. Limbo communicating causes lots of dropped presencing opportunities. For example, in earlier years we generated an unconscious habit of starting to speak when one of us was already leaving a room, so that wisps of sentences never got a chance to land. If you find yourself saying, "What?" a lot, you're probably not fully facing your partner.

We have gotten feedback over the years about our practice of turning toward each other, which is sufficiently unusual as to receive comments. One television show host remarked to us, "You look at each other when one of you is speaking? Do you do that all the time? You seem to actually be interested in what the other is saying." Yes, we replied, we actually find what the other is about to say of great interest and want to give our full attention. "Wow," he replied, "I've not seen that with other relationship experts who appear on our show."

When you open your posture, you become undefended. You signal to your body intelligence that you're open to input and connection. Your body posture lets your partner know that you are available even before either of you speaks. And if you *do* feel defensive, opening your posture lets a flow of bonding hormones circulate rather than the armored shield of adrenaline. You're setting the stage for deep presencing.

Easy, relaxed breathing signals safety to your whole being. Rather than the high, short breaths that precede a fight or the held breath of withdrawing, easy, open breathing creates flow and invitation. In the moments of potential misunderstanding, a deep breath or three shifts you to another track so that you're traveling together again.

The Truth Problem

In the original *Conscious Loving* we gave a lot of attention to speaking honestly. Over the years we have called this practice telling the microscopic truth or speaking unarguably. At first, when we enthusiastically shared truth-telling processes with clients and workshop participants, they seemed to frequently respond with a mixture of fear and dread. We were also astounded to see hundreds of people choose to withhold and get distant from their partners rather than step into those moments of facing reality and being vulnerable. Why would this be so? So many of us have accumulated heavy baggage attached to the word *truth*. The deep association seems to be that truth equals getting in trouble, and those memory traces run deep in people's systems, carried by their fear circuitry. It's important to be able to share what is most deeply true, but how do you even find your honesty when you've learned that telling the truth gets you ridiculed, rebutted, or punished?

We have come to see a whole new perspective about telling the truth that has emerged from the practice of presencing while speaking. Rather than an exercise in morality or competing worldviews, speaking becomes more an experience of matching or describing. We've learned to let the words paint a picture of inner experience rather than defending a fact or an event.

Shifting to matching and describing frees up your whole body and mind to delight in the joy of expressing. When you notice yourself with curiosity and do your best to paint a picture of your experience for another, you're presencing while you talk. We now call this speaking from *discovery*, because you do actually discover new connections and new aspects of yourself and your partnership when you presence while sharing. Here are some common phrases that show up when people learn to speak from discovery:

Here's what I'm noticing . . .
I'm experiencing . . .
I just had the thought . . .
I wonder if this is connected to what happened earlier?
As I'm thinking of that interaction, I'm noticing a feeling emerging.

Speaking from discovery has become one of the most fulfilling aspects of our relationship. Every day both of us share what is emerging, and in the presence of each other's curiosity and Full-Spectrum Presence, we continue to discover the vast inner frontier of consciousness and deeper emergence. We wish that everyone in the world could bask in the bliss of unedited speaking. You may have had dreams of flying as a child (and in the present as well)—we did. Speaking from discovery is as close to catching the currents and soaring as humans can experience without wings.

You can shift from fear-driven concealing to speaking from discovery by getting curious and doing your best to describe rather than defend. Each interaction gives you another chance to choose wonder and to share openly. Each time you describe, you add more feathers to your wings. You grow your ability to be here in the energy of the moment and enjoy the endless possibilities of intimacy with yourself and others.

Listening with Presence

Full-Spectrum Presencing influences your listening in profound ways. Couples have been taught versions of active listening in books and courses for years—practices that generally focus on the content, the words exchanged. It's important to get the details, especially of an agreement or meeting time. But presencing expands your ability to resonate with your partner in more and more harmonious ways. As you open your posture, loop your awareness, and turn on your deep curiosity, you begin to hear the deeper aspects of your beloved's journey. You access his or her dreams and memories, listen for what is emerging, and co-create a future based on the deep contact that presencing builds. Our conversations these days blend deep feelings, new discoveries, images from the day, jokes, new research that interests us, and more. Your presence-full listening continues to weave meaning and creation through your days. Rather than undoing your weaving every day (as Penelope did in secret at night waiting for Odysseus's return), you add layer after layer of shared experience to the right-now richness of your exchanges. Your contact deepens, gets juicier, delights you more and more. Presence becomes as much a nutrient as what you choose to eat every day.

The Rewards for Practicing Presence

What can you expect from practicing presencing over time? Synchronicity increases. You'll find your mate deeply in tandem with you about daily choices and big decisions. We've found that we regularly speak what the other has just been thinking. When one of us is traveling, we often find that we pick up our phones to call each other at exactly the same time, whether we're several states apart or around the world from home. Creative ideas spark simultaneously and find their way to completion with ease. Don't mistake this for two robots uttering the same script. The experience is more of two whole spaces resonating, just as two voices in harmony create a new and unique sound together.

When we wrote *Conscious Loving,* we wrote a subtitle that seemed radical at the time: *A Way to Be Fully Together Without Giving Up Yourself.* Now, a couple of decades later, we can confirm that learning how to not lose yourself is just the beginning. You can feel connected all the time, whether you're in the same place or not, waking or sleeping. Your practice of presencing generates a palpable space between: the "we" field of expanding creative flow. The we space begins to include others and spread to anyone who has contact with you. Your love and harmony inspire deeper connection and creativity for others around you.

People always know where we are at a conference or a retreat because that's where they can hear the most laughter. Ongoing presencing simply creates more fun. You get busy having a great time and finding more and more ways to enjoy being together. Gay creates spontaneous dances for Katie because he knows how much she treasures a good body joke. For example, he'll burst spontaneously into an exaggerated "dance to spring," complete with leaps, bounds, and operatic gestures until Katie is rolling around in giggles. Katie might find a fabulous cartoon or article featuring word play and read it out loud to Gay. Each of us is continuously open to more ways we can delight each other and add to the daily experience of beauty and joy.

Robert, a longtime practitioner of our work, describes a new game he and his wife, Conny, developed that adds presencing to the common "love ya, babe" shorthand that couples often settle into rather than expanding intimacy:

> Conny and I have created a new game about the phrase "I love you." We frequently say that to each other during every day. It is a reminder to us that we really do love each other—words that neither of us heard very frequently, if at all, as we were growing up. So sometimes when one of us says, "I love you," the other will ask, "How much?!" The objective then is to make the answer as wildly big as we feel up to in the moment. An example:
>
> "I love you."
>
> "How much?!"
>
> "More than all the molecules of water in the ocean that surrounds our property—and that's a lot!"
>
> The key is the last few words—"and that's a lot." We always finish with that. Sometimes we challenge each other on the "bigness" of our imagination depending on how we judge the answer—and ask the other to try again!

Easy solutions for issues or daily problems emerge from deepened presence. Your harmony and Loop of Awareness replace conflict and control; they remove the static of looking for what's wrong and trying to improve each other. You find you've got lots of free time and also notice when communications are beginning to go askew before they turn completely wonky. Your intuition extends to catching repairs on the front end rather than the catastrophic end. Maintenance becomes a game of keeping life humming at the most delightful level rather than digging out of one hole after another. Robert describes how he and Conny have changed their responses to problems:

> We are able to examine our behaviors more easily and without as much charge, noticing what we do and being willing to discuss what we notice without making each other wrong in the process. The key here is a heightened sensitivity that we are continuing to develop with each other—a higher level of noticing and awareness for and about each other. This is tied in with a leap forward in the appreciation we have for each other and the many appreciations we express for each other. We now relax into acknowledging and expressing our differences—celebrating them too—giving them space to coexist.

Creating Variety with Presencing

Scientists have recently documented a process they call pattern interrupt: the power of changing one small thing in an existing system to change the whole. Presencing continuously interrupts attention ruts, interaction patterns, and inherited programs. As you give your rich awareness to you and then shift to noticing your partner or your environment, you interrupt filters and habits in a friendly way. You get to expand your perception and move from one point of view to another. You get smarter as you let new neurons fire together and loosen long-standing attention habits.

Longtime couples are famous for complaining that they know everything about their partners. They've heard all the stories, can finish each other's sentences, and often assume that they've reached the bottom of a dry well. Simply shifting attention regularly refills the well with interest. Loop of Awareness generates discovery, and interrupting perception habits expands your ability to look for what's new, what's emerging. There are great comforts in the familiar, but just sitting in your favorite chair every day makes both it and you more lumpy. Think for a moment of the patterns you could predict in your parents' interactions and how you often knew what was going on before they said anything. That ability to perceive can be expanded by changing the way you give your attention.

Presencing is sexy. Really. You *know* when someone gives you their full presence, and you know the swoony sensual opening that streams from those moments. Imagine feeling entirely comfortable and easy in your body all the time so your attention is completely free to dance with your partner as well as you. You don't need to get approval to feel lovable, so you're open to spontaneity, to deeply feeling and sensing both you and your partner. That's sexy because all your energy is coursing throughout your body and rippling out through your skin, eyes, and touch. Your partner always looks brand new to you because you're becoming brand new to yourself through your presencing. Your curiosity about what's happening now and how you are now and what's wanting to emerge now—that's juicy. Being bathed in another's full attention—priceless. When Gay comes into the room, Katie feels thrilled all over again and has the thought *I can't believe how lucky I am to be married to THIS man.* Upping the wow factor in your relationship can continue throughout life. That never needs to wane if you practice presencing.

Presencing provides resources to flow with change, which seems to accelerate in many ways in later life. Many people seem to get more crystallized as they accumulate years, settling into both physical and mental habits, such as eating the same thing at the same time every day, holding on to old beliefs about "the way things used to be" in the imaginary better past. They give in to gravity and eventually disappear. In close relationship, holding on to the past can be particularly painful, since physical changes are inevitable and often unpredictable. Presencing promotes gratitude for the perfection of this moment, this interaction, the richness of fully being here and exchanging energy with you, your beloved, and the world. Presencing makes you more transparent to life's pageant, celebrating the parade while also letting it pass through the open space at your center.

Presencing allows you to make new connections between events, actions, qualities, and possibilities, which is a primary component of intelligence. Giving your attention to your experience and then focusing out on the world and others weaves new neural connections that keep your brain growing and resilient. Presencing is a kind of consciousness conditioning. Just as physical exercise keeps jumping higher on the list of Must Dos for those at midlife and beyond, flexing your consciousness expands the field of exploration and youths you rather than aging you.

Presencing promotes genuine response-ability. In the flow of full awareness, you notice new perspectives, new possibilities, and new actions you can take now. You see new aspects of your mate and your friends. Your genuine attention makes them more beautiful and more valuable to themselves and to you. The moment of light focused on a jewel illuminates more facets, and so it is with your attention. Routines and reactions dissolve with the simple act of shifting your awareness. We've heard thousands of exclamations like this one: "Oh! I totally didn't see that possibility until now."

People often form a narrow lens about relationship possibilities and then forget that their perception is the movie camera framing the scene in which they act. Imagine going to a movie where the camera angle or aperture never changed. How long would you stay in the theater? But people in close relationship or singles wanting to form a relationship often don't examine the movie they're dreaming up. The kind of Full-Spectrum Presencing we're inviting you into allows you to create and re-create the most vibrant and fulfilling movie you can imagine. Your wonder-infused perception connects you to your deepest intuition and invites others to expand to their fullest aliveness.

Others get inspired being in the same room with Full-Spectrum Presencing. We often get the feedback after public presentations that people respond to the laughter, see the easy exchanges, and feel the respect and caring. Though they often can't give words to what it is, they say, "I want what you have." This is how you get there, through the practice of presencing. We've both meditated every day now for several decades. The practice at the beginning was full of squirms and chaotic thoughts, falling asleep, and all kinds of distracting physical sensations. But from the very beginning something else started, a kind of stillness at the core and open, breezy flow inside. The practice expanded those qualities and more, so that the journey itself became a source of nourishment. Presencing is like that. Even if you're awkward at first, your practice will get easier. We've found that the other person receives the intention to love and presence even if the delivery isn't perfect.

The Big Reward for Presencing

Presencing expands play. In surveys about creating successful long-term relationships and in surveys about what singles most want in a mate, humor comes out consistently in the top five. Play doesn't even make the list. People think of play as a juvenile trait that gets sloughed off with adulthood. We've found play has taken first place over time in our interactions and in the exchanges of the couples we've coached.

Playing with personas and playing through issues replace control and conflict or working on problems. In *Conscious Loving* we outlined a sequence of moves that has proved remarkably reliable over these decades:

You withhold → you withdraw → you project

Most people have learned to conceal for one reason or another, often as a survival tactic. Concealing and withholding take measurable physical energy. The act of withholding removes you from right-now presence and connection. You withdraw to seal off the expression wanting to break through. From a withdrawn place, your partner starts looking different, starts appearing like the enemy or at least the source of the problem.

The ongoing practice of Full-Spectrum Presencing leads to this sequence instead:

You presence → you connect → you play

You bring your full awareness to what is happening inside you and what you can appreciate in another. The flow of awareness connects you deeply to your experience and to the continuum of experience and expression flowing through you and between you both. That exchange of attention creates something new: the play of energy, resonance, and appreciation. Creative impulses give rise to emergence, the co-creation of new contact games, new facets of possibilities, new aspects to appreciate.

Your reward for making these new moves is often immediate. For example, while we were working on this chapter we got an e-mail from a Canadian couple, Celeste and Michael, who gave us a perfect example of Full-Spectrum Presencing. Michael wrote:

> I was talking to Celeste about some ordinary household stuff when I noticed I was feeling a buzzy sensation in my chest and some dryness in my eyes. I paused to tune in and feel what those sensations were about, because they didn't really match what we were talking about. About two seconds after I tuned in to those sensations, I felt a welling up of appreciation for Celeste; I could feel how much love she had for me. Suddenly the words we were speaking to each other didn't really matter—it was the love underneath them that was important. I shared what I was feeling with Celeste and we ended up both holding each other, crying tears of joy.

In ordinary clock time their moment of Full-Spectrum Presencing was brief, but the magic of it doesn't depend on the amount of time you spend doing it. When you are in the present, you dissolve time and enter the infinite spaciousness of right-now connection. It's the only place where genuine intimacy can occur.

We have included detailed and effective presencing processes for both singles and couples in Appendix A: The Love Catalyst for Singles and The Love Catalyst for Couples. If you take the time to dive into these tools and integrate them as regular practices, you'll find a sweet and unexpectedly yummy result occurring, which we explain in the next chapter.

CHAPTER FOUR

The Best Sex Ever

"We're having the best sex we've ever had!"

That's the most frequent response we hear from people who try out the new tools you're learning in this book. We can certainly echo that in our own marriage. In the years since we turned 50, our own sexual experience has come to range between amazing and cosmic. We think the primary reason for the surge in great sex since midlife is that the present—this very moment—is incredibly sexy, and as you saw in Chapter Two, so is integrity. When you put these two potent, positive forces together in a relationship, you create a new force field around you in which your sexuality can thrive anew.

When two people in a relationship can step out from under, if only for a moment, the cloud of their past programming, they can kindle sexual energy again, even if it's been missing for years. We experienced that miraculous phenomenon in our own marriage, and we've witnessed it many times in our office and seminars. There comes a moment when two people see each other with fresh eyes—they catch a quick glimpse of the creative essence of the other person, the one they fell in love with. Suddenly they feel again the powerful forces that first drew them together.

Falling in Love Again . . . with Yourself

Getting to that moment requires that you first fall in love with *yourself* in a new way. To make beautiful love with a beloved, learn to make beautiful love with yourself . . . 24 hours a day if possible.

What does it mean to make love to oneself 24 hours a day?

- It means greeting your moment-by-moment experience with graceful ease.

- It's operating your body so you feel waves of natural, positive energy when you move and breathe.

- It's loving as much as you can from wherever you find yourself.

- It means being attuned to your own needs and feelings with the same degree of sensitive awareness you want from your beloved.

The more you do all those things, the more you feel a flow of positive energy inside you. There's nothing sexier than walking through life feeling that sensation of aliveness with every step and every breath you take. Even better, it's catching. That's why the best and first thing you can do to ignite a great sexual relationship with another person is to fall madly in love with yourself.

The second important thing you can do is embrace a revolutionary idea about sex and how to communicate about it.

The Sexual Universe

As we noted earlier, we all got here through an act of sex—that's where it all starts for all of us. Everything else is a spin-off and an elaboration. As humans, we're not finished evolving yet either. We're all still in a process of sexual evolution, and nobody knows where it all will lead. Here, though, and now, you can take charge of your own sexual revolution with a new and unusual leap of consciousness. So, right now, take another moment to savor the absolute pervasiveness of sex and sexual energy in life.

It's not possible to think an unsexual thought. Even though we may be pondering something that seems nonsexual, such as a math concept, those seemingly abstract thoughts are not so abstract at all. They are occurring in a wet environment, each one fired by an electrical jolt—just like the original wet and electric event that got us here. Everything is sexual, because that's where we all come from.

There is a remarkable payoff for embracing the unusual point of view that everything is ultimately sexual. It opens up the possibility that you might be able to imbue every moment of life with the good feelings usually reserved only for the act of physical love-making. With some practice, you might even be able to feel like you're making love all the time, walking down a busy street in Manhattan or making an inspired soup in the kitchen.

What if our natural birthright as human beings is to feel as good inside ourselves, in every moment, as we do when we're making passionate love with a beloved? Extend that question into the area of relationships: what if our natural birthright as sexual beings gives us permission to feel the sweet flow of essential connection in every moment of our closest relationships, the same flow as when we're physically making love?

We began to ask those kinds of big questions early in our relationship. They seemed outrageously bold at the time, and actually still do. We're not finished answering them yet, either. Now in our 60s, we have better sex than we had in our 30s, 40s, or 50s. We like to think anything's possible. It would delight us immensely if the trend continues into our 70s and later. If that happens, you can bet we'll let you know!

Now let's make all this very practical. If you are willing to embrace the possibility that every moment of life can be sweetened with a milder version of the same energy that, intensified, happens in lovemaking, you are ready for the particulars of how to make that happen.

That Salad Was the Best Foreplay We Ever Had

At least that's what one couple told us, and it's worth hearing how they got to that unusual comment. The problem they brought to us was that Rob had a tendency to move through a predictable routine in the bedroom—minimal foreplay, just a few practiced strokes on previously mapped-out areas of Sally's sensitivity, then a missionary mount with the same rhythms from insertion to climax. After years of pointing out the flaws in Rob's technique to him, Sally had sunk into silent resentment for years before making the courageous step of asking for help.

We've developed many tools and techniques to help couples break through long-term logjams in the bedroom and elsewhere in the house. Some of those techniques would likely be considered unorthodox by the mainstream, but we've been around long enough to know that what's unorthodox one year may be the industry standard a few years down the line. In that spirit, let us proceed to the subject of salad as an erotic experience.

One of the high aims of relationship coaching is to do something right away that will shake up the habitual routines of the relationship. As we pointed out in Chapter One, creativity is the great mega-solution for increasing love after midlife. For that reason, we always do our best to give a couple an experience that's completely outside the context of everyday life, something they've never done before. In the case of Rob and Sally, we asked them to make a salad together. The astonished look on their faces told us that we had just succeeded in shifting the context. One moment they were stuck in a rut together; the next moment they're having an adventure together.

When we work with couples who live far away and can't come in on a weekly basis, we often use a format we call a One-Day Intensive. We work with them all day long, including having a working lunch together. This format packs about six months of transformational change into a short period of time. After a One-Day Intensive, we follow up with sessions usually done by videoconference.

We brought Rob and Sally out to the kitchen and set out the makings of a salad: several types of greens, carrots, endive, radishes, string beans, olive oil, and lemon. (One of us is allergic to tomatoes and both of us to vinegar, hence the absence of these two typical salad ingredients.)

We didn't give them any specific instructions beyond "Would you two please make the salad together?" We were keenly interested in watching how they went about it on their own, and as is almost always the case, the way they started making their salad was exactly what was wrong with their lovemaking.

Right away Sally plunged into making the salad, while Rob hung back looking helplessly in our direction, as if wanting us to tell him what to do next. We just continued laying out the other lunch items.

Rob picked up a radish, but before he could do anything with it, Sally said, "Wash your hands first. Then chop those carrots."

Rob let out a sigh and followed her orders. He began chopping carrots, slowly and deliberately, whacking the cutting board with the knife in an operatically loud manner.

Here was a microcosm of themes we'd been working on with them before lunch. Rob complained of Sally "always being bossy," while Sally served up her countercomplaint: without her constant guidance, Rob would just stand around "like a potted plant, waiting for somebody to water him."

We asked them to pause from the salad for a moment while we shared our observations with them. "Notice how those themes are right here in the making of salad," Katie said. "No doubt they're right there in your lovemaking too." Their heads bobbed together; they knew what she was talking about.

"So, would you be willing to try something completely different?" Gay asked.

They looked mystified, but they said, "Yes."

Katie said, "We'd like you to make a new salad, but this time we'd like you to make it just like the way you'd like to make love."

The look on their faces went past mystified to dumbfounded. "What do you mean?"

"What's one way you'd like your lovemaking to be?" Gay asked. "One quality you'd like it to have?"

Sally said, "Playful."

"Okay, then, when you make your salad, focus on playing as you do it."

"What about him? What if Rob's not playful?"

"Good question. You could play on your own, and not think about what Rob's doing. Or you could ask him, 'Are you willing to make our salad playfully?'"

"Rob," Sally said, "will you make a salad playfully with me?"

"I don't know exactly what you're talking about, but yeah, okay."

We invited them to make a few playful moves with their salad ingredients. Sally put a radish on the edge of the bowl, then rolled it down into the center of the bowl with a flick of her finger. Rob stuck a spoon into the lemon and oil dressing that Sally had mixed and let a dollop fall onto the avocado he'd added. Sally picked up some greens and started chopping them with comic ferocity, like a samurai wielding a sword. Rob responded by swooping his arm around like an airplane and dropping a handful of sunflower seeds into the mix.

Already there was color in their cheeks that hadn't been there before. We invited them to add a new intention. "What's another quality you'd like your lovemaking to have? Rob, what's one of yours?"

"Nobody criticizes anybody."

It's common for people to express themselves in negative terms, as what they *don't* want. We've found that it's helpful to get beyond the "don't" to the "do." In other words, what does Rob want to experience instead of criticism?

"Rob, that's what you don't want, but what would you like to feel and see instead of criticism? What's the positive thing you want to feel?"

"Like we're appreciating each other."

"Excellent. So, get that started right now. Tell Sally one thing you appreciate about her." This request caught him by surprise;

like many people, he had become so focused on the negative that he had trouble conceiving of the positive. After a moment he said, "I think you make good decisions."

"Thank you," Sally said.

"How about you, Sally? What's something you appreciate about Rob?"

Sally said, "I appreciate how you've always showed up for the kids' soccer and skating."

"Really good," Katie said. "So, we've got two positive intentions: playful and appreciative. Put your attention back on making the salad, and this time make it playfully and appreciatively. Play with it, and be sure you pause to appreciate as often as you can."

Twenty minutes later we sat down to eat together, starting with a very unusual salad. Sally and Rob had filled four round plates with chopped greens arranged into the shape of a face, with radishes for eyes and string beans for eyebrows. Julienned carrots were strategically placed to look like blushes on the cheeks of the salad. A piece of string cheese curved upward at the ends served as the smile on the face of the salad. It was definitely the most playful salad we'd ever seen, and we gave them lavish appreciation for it.

We didn't talk about sex specifically after lunch. Instead we helped them implement the qualities of "playful and grateful" into the rest of our work together that day. Then they left, and what happened later that night inspired them to report back to us that making the salad "was the best foreplay we ever had." It had led to a playful, appreciative, and extensive session of, as Rob put it, "rolling and tumbling like we'd never even done in our whole lives."

Playful and grateful are two excellent intentions for lovemaking. They certainly worked to turn Rob and Sally's relationship around. Don't stop there, though. There are dimensions of sexuality you can explore later in life that take you into the higher reaches of human awareness. These dimensions are not easily available to us up until midlife; after 45 or so, they are much easier to attain. To understand why this is so, take a leap with us from salad to metaphysics.

The Practical Metaphysics of Sexuality

The wizards of science tell us that there are three levels of reality: mass, energy, and space. Translating that into practical terms, it means that we humans can experience three levels of reality at any given moment:

- The physical body
- The energy body
- The space body

We're all familiar with the physical body, the one we have to feed, wash, and do our best to occupy when we're making love. The physical body has its areas of exquisite sensitivity, but at the same time its pleasures are finite. Touch the same pleasurable place too much or too often and it stops feeling good. By contrast, the pleasures of the energy body and the space body are infinite, at least in our explorations so far.

The energy body cannot be seen, only felt. It comprises all the hums, vibrations, currents, and sweeps of sensation you can feel in the universe inside you. In our experience, most people are not very aware of their energy bodies until they put some conscious attention into exploring the inner world. The same is true for the space body.

Practically speaking, your space body is all the territory inside you where you feel open to loving and being loved. The space body is more elusive to feel than the energy body, and usually requires even more dedicated focus to become aware of it. For example, think of looking out into space at the stars in the sky. The stars, with their twinkle and shine, tend to capture our attention, making it easy to overlook how much pure space there is between them. Science tells us that there is proportionately as much pure space between the solid elements inside our physical bodies as there is between the stars in the nighttime sky. However, it usually doesn't feel that way; in fact, it often feels very crowded inside us, as if we are constructed less like the spacious universe and more like sausage wrapped in a too-tight casing.

The reason it feels so jam-packed inside ourselves is simply that we haven't known how to become aware of our energy body and space body. For most of us, our formal schooling does not include a course that, in our view, should be part of the curriculum from kindergarten forward. In our dream future, children will get an hour's training every day, right alongside the multiplication tables and the names of the state capitals, in a course called something like "Body Intelligence: How to Deal with Your Feelings and Other Important Aspects of Your Inner World."

Imagine what a world it would be if we all knew how to deal effectively at times when we're scared, sad, or angry. Imagine a world in which politicians, thanks to all their early training in body intelligence throughout elementary school, know how to solve problems without making anybody wrong. A look at the current political environment pretty much anywhere in the world is enough to see that this skill would be useful globally. Instead, generations of children get no training in the essentials of communication, but spend weeks memorizing the state capitals.

Here's a piece of dialogue we've never heard in all our years of counseling couples:

Partner One: I'm going to ask you one more time—what is the capital of South Dakota?

Partner Two: Uh, I don't remember.

Partner One: Okay, I've had it with you—get your stuff and clear out now!

However, we can definitely attest, based on hundreds of conversations in our office, that dialogue like the following goes on frequently between couples:

Partner One: What are you feeling right now?

Partner Two: Uh, I don't know.

Partner One: Well, are you angry? Scared? Sad? Happy? You've got to be feeling something.

Partner Two: Uh, I don't know.

The lack of self-knowledge and sensitivity to the inner world is extremely costly to relationships, whether at home or at large in the world. It's actually easy to learn how to know if you're mad, sad, scared, or happy; it just takes a little practice in developing the necessary sensitivity. For example, just as a kindergartner can learn to tell the difference between orange and yellow, the ability to discern the difference between fear and hunger is equally simple. It just requires the acquisition of a particular type of awareness.

Fine-Tuning Your Receiver

At midlife and thereafter, one of the most significant things you can do for your overall well-being is to devote yourself to becoming even more sensitive than you already are to the messages your body is sending you. Your maturity gives you the ability to put things in perspective based on your life experiences. You're more sensitive; you see things more clearly than you did in earlier decades. At the same time, and through no fault of your own, you're in a time of life when bodies begin falling apart at an escalating clip. You're up against that inexorable force the physicists call the Three Laws of Thermodynamics, which, summarized in simple terms, go something like this:

1. You can't win.
2. You can't break even.
3. You can't get out of the game.

The reason for this bleak picture is simple, so say the scientists, but it's often a little hard to look at without wincing: they tell us the universe is proceeding toward an ultimate heat death about five billion years down the line. Even harder to face is that everything is expanding away from everything else at a speed that's barely possible to comprehend. It's an illusion to think things are falling apart; what they're actually doing is *flying* apart.

Nobody at present knows where our expanding juggernaut of a universe is all heading. For example, some hopeful scientists have suggested that after the universe has expanded into nothingness it will do a cosmic flip, re-form, and come back in some other configuration. If their time estimates are accurate and it actually takes five billion years for the universe to fizzle out, we'll have to cultivate some patience to wait for the turnaround to occur. In the meantime, what does the universe flying apart have to do with your love life?

Here's the practical use you can make of this unusual situation humans are in at midlife and older. First, take a moment to appreciate the dilemma: here we are at a time in our lives when we have grown in astounding, unpredictable ways based on our life experience up through our 40s. We know a lot more about ourselves, other people, and the world around us than we did earlier in our lives. But now, just when we should be rejoicing in the radiance of our wisdom, we encounter around every corner the lurking presence of the Three Laws.

"Once I was taking a walk with a friend of mine, an M.D. of many decades' experience," Gay says. "I mentioned that I'd been having pain in my left knee and that I was thinking about getting arthroscopic surgery to fix the crackles, pops, and crunches that accompanied my formerly smooth gait. My doctor friend nodded and said matter-of-factly, 'Yep, we're getting to that age now when bodies start to fall apart.'"

After midlife it dawns on us that we're just like the universe itself—expanding like crazy, sometimes even feeling like we're about to come apart at the seams, while at the same time extending the reach of our consciousness further than it's ever been before. In the meantime, while we're enjoying the lofty sweep of our mature thoughts, forces are conspiring to make our knees ache, our memory fade, and our midriffs swell with fat. As one of our clients put it, "It's like I'm getting better and worse every day, all at the same time." In the midst of that seemingly unsolvable dilemma, what can any of us do?

The very best thing we've found is to turn the experience of your aging body into a spiritual path of its own. To do that, you commit yourself to a program of continuous worship, devoted to tuning and fine-tuning your vehicle. If you're going to make the most of the second half of your life, you're going to have to contend with the Three Laws of Thermodynamics. It will take every ounce of your courage and creativity to get into harmony with this powerful force and turn it to your advantage.

The payoff for your dedication is immense: the ability to surf on waves that are pulling a lot of people under. In practical reality, your sexuality is also the beneficiary of coming to your aging process as a spiritual practice. To produce reliable magic in your lovemaking, the most effective thing you can do long term is to get dedicated to a program of fine-tuning your own body first. You can tune up your physical body at the gym or on a brisk walk around the neighborhood, but fine-tuning your energy and space body requires a different type of exercise.

Making love with the energy body and the space body is the real possibility of sexuality at midlife and beyond. You're more sensitive in your energy body, yet at the same time you're more resilient. You've been through more, so you can go beyond the physical more easily.

There's no limit to the amount of conscious awareness you can turn on in your body. Personally, we simply cannot believe the difference in our lovemaking since we committed ourselves to learning to navigate the inner world of the energy body and the space body. You'll find remarkable activities later in the book that facilitate your ability to navigate mass, energy, and space, but for now, take a moment to open the conversation with a moment of dedicated self-awareness.

Right now, right where you are, notice your energy body. Deliberately scan yourself from the top of the head on down through to the soles of your feet; simply feel what you feel, for no reason other than to exercise your natural awareness. First notice the overall sense of life happening inside you. What are the sensations you can feel at this moment that let you know you are alive? Feel the hums, buzzes, waves, and pulsations that are happening inside you and all of us at every moment. If you can't yet feel the specifics of any of those sensations, simply tune in to the general sense of aliveness in your body.

Now scan your space body: notice everywhere you can feel the vast inner ocean of pure awareness—not awareness of any particular thing but just the awareness itself. Do you feel a sense of open spaciousness everywhere or nowhere? Either answer is fine, and so is everything in between. You're on a benign search expedition, an adventure to feel the maximum amount of spacious energy and inner ease. To make the adventure have the very highest stakes, use our practical definition of the space body: how much openness you feel to loving and letting yourself be loved.

In a very real sense—in a way you can actually feel in your body—love and space are essentially the same. If you love someone, you give that person the space to develop to his or her fullest capacity. If someone loves you, he or she gives you the same room to grow. It works the same way inside—to love and respect yourself is to give yourself space to grow to your highest creative expression, free of criticism, self-shaming, and all the other tools of the judging mind.

Loving and feeling the body quiets the mind and opens presencing in our lovemaking, where a vast territory opens up for potential creative exploration. After one of our seminars we got an e-mail from a couple who had awakened in this new territory and were starting to chart its pleasures:

> For us there has been a shift in consciousness, so that we now put an emphasis on the actual process of lovemaking rather than the final goal of orgasm. We are consciously choosing to share with each

other before lovemaking what we really want, which is connection and union, and to expand from the physical connection all the way to a spiritual one. We noticed a pattern, that one of us is usually more physically active, so we are developing strategies to involve both of us with our whole bodies during lovemaking (for example, making love standing up). We find these strategies as well as conscious breathing help enormously with having more energy evenly distributed in our bodies as opposed to concentrated around the genitals. We are still refining some breathing exercises, for example, synchronizing our breathing while we're making love. So far, most of our experiments have been exquisite!

This couple expresses an attitude we feel is important to the process: experimentation. By its very nature an experiment has an aspect of play built into it; you can't exactly predict the outcome. One of the charms of play is that it usually involves on-the-spot invention and improvisation. For example, improvisational theater groups, such as Second City in Chicago, perform dozens of experiments in the course of a performance, all intended to produce a certain result: a combination of wonder and laughter. There are big benefits for getting good at producing those results; many Second City comics have made the leap to television and movies from that platform.

There are big benefits from experiments in conscious lovemaking too, starting with the opportunity to turn up the volume on your Sensory Delight Channel. With some practice and conscious attention, though, you can go beyond even that—through the gateway of sensory pleasure into a new space of unity and connection with another person. It is a space that feels transcendental, more spirit than body. For us it doesn't happen every time, but it has certainly happened a great deal more in the years after 50 than it ever happened before. We like the trend! Now, if it so appeals, turn your attention to making that kind of lovemaking happen for you.

The Only Technique You Really Need

You will need only two things to begin:

- A willing partner
- Your natural gift of awareness, the ability to focus your attention on one thing and another

When you have your willing partner rounded up and your awareness turned on, here's a practice you can experiment with to take your lovemaking into the stratosphere. In our view, it's the only technique you really need to make big leaps toward the transcendental in your lovemaking. It's so simple and natural that it's probably a stretch even to call it a technique, but in spite of its ease in implementation, it has a great deal of power to it.

Instructions

1. When you first begin foreplay, tune in to your breathing and consciously slow it down a little. Aim for slow and easy in your breathing.

2. When you're feeling the pleasure of your slow breathing, begin to synchronize your breathing with light touch of your own invention. For example, take a slow, easy in-breath, and then stroke the side of your partner's face in synchrony with a long, slow out-breath. Vary the places you touch, focusing on coordinating slow, pleasurable breathing with slow, pleasurable touch.

3. After you've explored the pleasures of synchronizing your breathing with touch, shift to the deepest part of the practice: synchronizing your breathing with your partner's breathing. Let go of conscious touch for a few moments and focus solely on harmonizing your breathing with your partner's. As you are harmonizing with your partner's breathing, your partner is doing the same with

you. You are now in a Loop of Awareness together, joined in unity through sharing breath and consciousness.

4.   The technique is open-ended—you can forget all about it and then resume it dozens of times during your lovemaking. Coming back into conscious synchrony with your partner's breathing is one of the pleasures of the practice; it feels just as good the thousandth time as it does the first.

Here's a report from a couple in their 60s who rode this simple technique from the physical out into the infinite reaches of the spiritual:

Diane and I decided to try the synchronized breathing finally, and now we wish we hadn't waited so long to do it. We were in the backyard together when we first thought about doing it, so Diane said, "Let's start now." We were standing up hugging each other when we hooked up our breathing, and I bet we stood there a good ten minutes just slow-breathing together, holding each other tight and swaying like we were slow-dancing. After a while we kind of staggered into the bedroom and collapsed on the bed. Diane got the idea of undressing each other, so we started doing that while we were still synchronizing our breathing. It was an amazing experience, just undressing her. It was so sexy taking off her clothes slowly while coordinating each movement with my breathing. Every now and then while we were making love we'd come back to matching up our breathing. It would always take us into feeling more connected. Because we kept coming back to the breath we took probably twice as long to get to a climax. When we did, though, it blew the lid off anything we remember feeling before. Our breaths got longer and longer to accommodate the rising feelings, and when we finally had our orgasms they took us out into a place like being melted together hovering in space.

They got a taste of the full potential of the technique, deeply experiencing the pleasures of the physical while expanding out into the infinite reaches beyond boundaries. Realistically, you probably won't reach that exalted place every time, nor do we.

Once you feel it, though, you'll know it's there, even if you don't attain it every time. It becomes, like the moon, a feature that adds beauty to the world even if it only comes into its fullness now and then.

Enhancing Sex Throughout Life

Jim Selman, a friend of ours who is now in his 70s, published a blog a while back in *The Huffington Post,* listing seven reasons why sex is better later in life. In Jim's view, sex is better because:

- You're more patient than you were at earlier life stages.
- You're able to give and receive more fully.
- You have better conversations before, during, and after sex.
- You're less judgmental.
- You're able to be more present.
- You're about savoring the journey, not just arriving at the destination.
- You understand more about love than you did earlier in your life.

In reading Jim's list, we were struck by how all of the reasons rest on a single essential skill, one that is learnable: the ability to presence. For example, the quality of patience is the practical skill of focusing on what is happening in the present moment, rather than thinking we need to be some other place that fits our preconceived expectations. Likewise, to understand love is to hone the ability to be present for it, so that you give yourself the opportunity to receive its magnificence on every possible level, unfiltered by your past experiences and future expectations.

We've been exploring that territory for decades now, and we can tell you this: the more you practice presencing, the more love you can feel and express. Once you dedicate yourself to the life skill of being in this moment, you get two gifts. When you say to the universe, "Yes! I choose to live in the present moment!" you get the gift right away of a new sense of liberation in your being, a feeling of spacious ease. The burden of the past lifts off you, and the future-forecasting part of your mind quiets down.

The second gift sometimes doesn't feel like one. Once you taste the exhilarating space of presencing in this moment, you want to spend more time there. Check that—you want to spend *all* your time there. You can't yet, though; you haven't had enough practice. In other words, you'll start to realize just how much of the time you spend *not* being present. You'll catch yourself dozens of times each day caught up in useless replays of the past or future-frets about things you have absolutely no control over. Once you get beyond its initial irritations, though, the gift has the potential for enormous positive impact in your life. Basically, it turns every moment of life into an open space for rich experience. You're right there, open to receive and open to give, rather than filtering your experience through past conditioning or future fantasies. Your love-making is the great beneficiary. To discover how your day-to-day experience can feel like making love all the time, read on.

CHAPTER FIVE

Blame-Free
Relationships

Whether you are single or have a partner, you need to feel what it's like to breathe the exhilarating air of a relationship free from blame and criticism. It feels absolutely delicious, unlike anything we ever imagined. That's what we want for you. If you dedicate yourself to eliminating blame and criticism from your communications with people you care about, you open up an immense new space in which your creativity can flourish. The more your creativity flourishes, the less interest you have in wasting your newfound creative zest on blame and criticism.

There's a troublesome belief that keeps criticism and blame recycling in relationships. The belief: *If I can just criticize and blame my partner long enough and loudly enough, eventually he/she will get the message and stop doing things that bother me.* This type of thinking leads us to criticize someone for leaving socks on the floor 118 times, with the expectation that on the 119th time the person will suddenly change. In the course of helping people undo lifelong patterns of blame and criticism, we've unearthed a deeper and even more limiting belief many of us are operating from: *If I don't keep a steady stream of criticism aimed at people I care about, they will devolve into even worse versions of themselves.*

Marriage researcher John Gottman named four troublesome relationship patterns the "Four Horseman of the Apocalypse" because they signal doom for the relationship if allowed to continue. The four patterns are criticism, contempt, defensiveness, and withdrawal (e.g., sulking instead of communicating).

Criticism is often the first of the Horsemen to emerge as the relationship veers toward trouble, and it doesn't take long for criticism to become chronic. Soon chronic criticism hardens into contempt, which in turn leads to defensiveness and withdrawal as the relationship swerves further off course.

The Most Challenging—and Rewarding—Mountain

Averting this relationship apocalypse and creating a blame-free relationship is a feat of consciousness similar to the physical challenge of climbing Mt. Everest. It's rarefied air, but you can breathe it if you want. Be prepared, though, to put in some work to get there. Unlike the trek up Everest, you won't need any extra equipment or physical prowess. Your consciousness is your entire tool kit. Make no mistake, though: it's a challenge that can even stymie people who have performed amazing feats such as actually climbing Mt. Everest. We know this because we have worked with several world-class mountain climbers in relationship counseling.

One of those couples had come in because chronic criticism was eating up the intimacy between them. We were astonished to see a man who had climbed one of the world's highest peaks *without oxygen* begin to hyperventilate when we asked him to look his partner in the eye and make a commitment to her. He had breathed his way to the top of K2, but when he tried to say a simple sentence to his beloved he choked, gasped, and began panting in terror. The sentence that sent his breathing into spasms was: "I commit to ending blame and criticism in our relationship."

As his wave of panic subsided, we guided him back to normal breathing and helped him get his feet firmly planted on the ground again. When he was ready, he looked into his partner's eyes again.

Gay said, "Tell Lenore as simply as possible why you got so scared that your breathing ran away with you."

Here's what came tumbling out of Jacob's mouth: "I'm scared to stop criticizing you because it's how I push you away."

"But why push me away?"

"So you won't get hurt. So you won't have to face who I really am."

First, Lenore used logic on him: "But we've been together seven years," she said. "I know everything about you!"

Logic produced its usual dismal results. Jacob just shook his head. "No, you don't. The only way I can keep from infecting you is if I keep you at a distance somehow."

"Infecting me? With what?"

"With my poison, the poison that killed Marie."

There it was, the fear that fueled his resistance to commitment with Lenore. His first wife, Marie, had committed suicide four years into their marriage. Although her death had been nearly a decade earlier, it was still casting a pall over him. Jacob was obviously afraid that he would bring the same kind of plague into a new marriage.

Jacob had the classic problem, a stack of old thinking errors that was keeping him from experiencing intimacy in the present moment. Most communication problems are built on an illusion of false thinking, an error of logic similar to a broken piece of code in the depths of your computer's operating system.

There were two levels of thinking error Jacob had to clear up:

Error #1: I am poison.

Error #2: My poison contributed to my wife's death.

In other words, he had convicted himself of two crimes—both imaginary—and was serving out the sentence for them in the real world of his relationship with Lenore.

As we worked with him on these issues, he traced them down to a sense of shame he'd carried in him as long as he could remember. He described the bodily feeling of the shame as an unpleasant heat that spread from his calves up to his face.

But whose shame was it? As a therapist, when you hear someone say a particular emotion feels like it's "been there forever," you automatically wonder if it got there before the person even saw daylight. We now know that our mothers' experiences can affect us in utero. With approximately 60 percent of us unplanned and almost 50 percent unwanted or mistimed, according to research by the Guttmacher Institute, it's easy to see why many of us spend the first months of our existence trapped inside the influence of an unsettling stew of emotions. As it turned out, Jacob had been surrounded by shame long before he became Jacob. His parents were students in a conservative religious college when he was conceived, so there was plenty of shame coming at him from various directions as he made his presence in the world known.

Being born is like dropping into a party that's been going on for a long time before you got there. It takes you a while to learn the folkways of the new planet you're getting acquainted with, and some of the local customs can be very, very strange. You can imagine that Jacob's growing-up process had lots of rich opportunities for imbibing limiting beliefs about the nature of love and relationship. After a marriage that lasted three years, Jacob's parents split up and seldom spoke to each other again in their lives. Jacob eventually went to live with an aunt and uncle who had eight other children. For Jacob it was yet another party that had been going on long before he got there, another set of folkways to learn.

By the time Jacob met his first wife, Marie, he was already a criticism waiting to happen. He had lived inside so many layers of shame that he mistakenly came to believe that those feelings were part of his natural-born, intrinsic self. He needed to wake up to the real truth: his shame was actually none of his business.

We made an intervention that helped him shed his two limiting beliefs, along with 40 years of burdensome history.

Katie said, "Do you remember a family who lived next door when you were growing up?"

Puzzled, Jacob said, "Yeah. One family I remember, the Brunsons. I used to play with Jimmy Brunson sometimes. Why?"

"Do you remember anything about the house they lived in?"

He nodded. "It was a white ranch house."

"Okay, so think about this for a moment. If you had grown up next door, Jimmy Brunson's brother, you would have had a whole different experience, right?"

"Sure. For one thing, they had a horse, but they didn't let any of the other kids ride it."

"So imagine all the things that would be different if you'd grown up next door. You'd have a completely different set of problems, right?"

"Yes."

"Now feel the part of you that would still be exactly the same, even if you'd experienced a completely different set of experiences growing up."

We love this moment. If we communicate the idea just right, people will get a glazed, faraway look in their eyes as they feel their essential, pure consciousness, often for the first time. Pure consciousness has a vast stillness to it, a silence that often goes unnoticed, hidden behind the compelling dramas of our learned histories. Whether you stumble across your pure consciousness by accident or cultivate your awareness of it through years of meditation, it always has a refreshing newness to it. We're both longtime practitioners of meditation, with more than 40 years of daily practice behind us. Yet even though we've spent thousands of hours in meditation, it always feels fresh and new to drop into that experience of pure consciousness every day.

Jacob got a smile on his face as the point sank in.

Gay said, "Maybe *somebody* thought you were poison once upon a time, but that was *their* poison, not yours. It didn't really have anything to do with you—they would have felt that way about anybody who was in there. Give them back all that shame. It was their problem, not yours."

It's something many people have never considered: the biggest problems we struggle with are often not really *our* own problems. It was other people who were having a problem with Jacob's existence in the world, not Jacob. He wasn't even "Jacob" yet; he was just doing what developing babies do from conception to birth, while around him the storms of shame were raging. The feeling of shame that Jacob found so pervasive in his body, in all his actions, and in his relationships—"I feel like every cell in my body is poisoned with it"—was not even his own shame.

Guilt and shame are only useful if they cause us to change our behavior in positive ways, and only if they are administered in a light enough dose that they won't hang around as a permanent feature of our emotional and relationship life. For example, if you get caught by your mom with your hand in the cookie jar, you're likely to feel some guilt or shame. That's the normal human response. The mosquito-nip of guilt or the squirmy feeling of shame is there to remind you not to poach forbidden cookies again. If the dose of guilt or shame you're administered is appropriate, you move on from the situation having learned from it. You move on without carrying such a burden of guilt and shame in your body that it causes you to think you've done something wrong at all times, no matter what you're doing.

In Jacob's case, he got a much bigger dose than usual, and he got it from the early moments of his origin. It was other people who were feeling shame about him, even before he took his first breath.

"When you've felt all that old shame as long as you have, it probably feels permanent, but can you also feel how it's not really your problem?" Gay asked Jacob. "It was somebody else's feeling of guilt and shame, not yours. You didn't do anything wrong."

We saw the burden lift off Jacob before our eyes. There's a certain look people get when they have this stunning awareness, a combination of wonder and relief, as a wise part of them suddenly realizes, *I don't need to take it personally. They would have felt that way about anybody. It's as if I inherited a way of thinking about myself along with my hair color and height. I walked into a guilt and shame party, and that was the only party in town at the time. Now I can see the possibility of creating a whole new party that I design.*

We sent Jacob and Lenore out for a walk to put their feet on the new perceptual ground Jacob's exploration had opened for them. Jacob's breath had deepened and relaxed, and he commented on

Lenore's hair as they were opening the door. He said, "Did you just get a new hairstyle? I like it!" Lenore giggled with delight, as Jacob had never noticed her hair changes before. They left whispering and holding hands.

Ending the Addiction

Most people we work with, even those who are extremely motivated to change their behavior, at first find it quite a challenge to eliminate blame and criticism from their relationship repertoire. The motivation comes easy once they realize how destructive blame and criticism actually are, but then comes the truly heroic task of doing the work. One of our clients put it this way: "After we started paying attention to criticizing each other, it was like looking out into a garden and suddenly seeing all these weeds that had been growing there all the time without us realizing it."

Fortunately, you don't have to solve the problem of blame and criticism one "weed" at a time. The weeding goes much easier once you spot the first one. All you need to do is catch yourself in mid-criticism *one time*, and replace the criticism with a sincere statement of authentic feeling. That's enough to break the spell of negativity cast by the old pattern. We've seen this with hundreds of couples: all it takes is one moment of changing in mid-sentence from criticism—"What on earth is wrong with you?"—to something like "I'm feeling stuck. I wonder how I keep getting into this same situation with you?"

On the surface it seems like a simple shift to make, and it is, but getting to the point of making that shift takes a heroic feat of awareness. We believe the main reason it's such a challenge—as we learned from our own early struggles to clear blame and criticism from our relationship—is that the pattern is a form of drug addiction.

Let's look at the facts. Criticism and blame are two of the worst ways ever invented to get people to change their behavior. In 40 years of relationship counseling we've never heard anyone make this kind of remark: "Finally all those years of daily criticism by my partner paid off! I decided to stop drinking!" What we usually hear goes more like this: "After all those years of daily criticism by my partner, I decided to move out."

The reason blame and criticism don't change behavior is simple: it's not their *purpose*. One of the big human delusions is that if we criticize someone enough, he or she will finally change. This delusion gets established the same way affection for slot machines does: sometimes we get a payoff. In other words, one day we're busily criticizing someone when they finally decide to change. It deludes us into thinking the criticism has finally worked.

Since criticism and blame almost never bring about the desired change, what is the actual purpose of them? In blunt language, the main purpose of blame and criticism is to get a fix—a microscopic dose of one of the most potent drugs of all, adrenaline. Known by its scientific name, *epinephrine,* adrenaline fires off in our systems when we aim blame and criticism at someone. Even in small doses it is extremely powerful and highly addictive. The central component of human adrenaline is so potent that a tiny taste of it will make monkeys do high-speed laps around their cages for hours. Rats will press a bar with manic enthusiasm to give themselves microscopic doses of adrenaline, and they'll keep on doing it until they keel over dead. It's powerful stuff, and we all home-brew it in the tiny steam pots of two small glands atop our kidneys.

For two glands that don't even weigh an ounce, our adrenals produce a chemical that plays a very large role in human affairs. Painful, repetitive relationship drama is one of the main outcomes of adrenaline addiction. Since almost everything from the boudoir to the battlefield has to do with relationship drama, the destructive effects of adrenaline addiction can be seen everywhere.

Human beings and other adrenaline-producing creatures (which includes almost everybody who walks, crawls, flaps, or flies) didn't produce adrenaline originally to create painful relationship dramas. Adrenaline evolved in order to help us *escape* painful relationship dramas, such as being eaten. Adrenaline is designed literally to help us "run for our lives." If that doesn't work, the energy of adrenaline also helps us fight back. Back in the dawn of human evolution, adrenaline came in very handy. You needed a strong chemical to jolt you out of your sleep and get you ready to throw stones at a saber-toothed tiger at the mouth of the cave. Now, a few millennia later, we still produce about the same amount of adrenaline as we did back in the cave days, but it's mostly metaphorical tigers we deal with.

Enter relationship drama. To occupy the time freed up by having fewer actual tigers to fight, modern-day humans create relationship dramas of an intensity and scale that make the days of dealing with actual saber-toothed tigers seem like a luxury.

It all starts at home, though; for most of us, the major arenas for adrenalized interactions are the kitchen and the bedroom.

Why would human beings get into the habit of injecting unnecessary adrenaline into our bloodstreams by criticizing and blaming? The reason is that adrenaline relieves boredom, fatigue, and despair, all of which are daily realities to many people in relationships. If you were a cave person sitting around feeling bored, tired, and bummed out, the whole morass of bad mood would disappear in a flash if you heard a tiger's roar outside. Adrenaline takes less than a second to hit your bloodstream. Your mind focuses and your muscles tighten; you're ready to go.

In the same way, if you are a married person sitting around feeling bored, tired, and depressed, you can jolt yourself temporarily out of the low mood by administering a dose of adrenaline. The simplest way to do that is to trigger an argument. Actually, it doesn't need to rise to the level of an argument; all it takes is one sharp or unconscious comment. The brain sends out an alarm and administers a squirt of adrenaline: "We're under attack. Run, fight, freeze, or faint—pick one!"

The stimulating effects of drugs such as caffeine and nicotine on mind and body are widely known. Both of us had parents who were best approached in the morning only after they had their second cup of coffee in one hand and a cigarette in the other. The effects of adrenaline are less widely known, but it's certainly a much stronger drug than either caffeine or nicotine.

If criticism doesn't work, why do people come back to it over and over? Blaming and criticizing release that hit of adrenaline that bodies crave in the absence of another kind of juiciness. The instantaneous hit, the momentary rush of being right, overrides the realization that you're riding the same roller coaster over and over, expecting to get off at a different place.

Our Own Struggles

Not surprisingly, then, criticizing and blaming each other was a habit we found harder to eliminate than ordinary addictions we'd kicked, such as nicotine and sugar. Gay was addicted to cigarettes all through college, but when he finally decided to quit smoking, it took only three days of really unpleasant body sensations before the addiction disappeared. That was 40 years ago and he's never had the urge to smoke again. Compared to quitting blame and criticism, kicking tobacco addiction was a breeze. Even with dedicated focus on eliminating blame and criticism, it still took us many years to stop the habit.

But stop it we did. We focused on eliminating blame and criticism relentlessly in the '80s, and one day in the '90s we woke up and realized we hadn't said a critical word to each other in many months. We've stretched out our no-blame streak quite a bit since those days.

Ending blame and criticism completely may seem far out of reach, especially if you've been in a relationship where the level of negativity was or is so high you can feel the pain of it just by recalling the interactions. It felt far out of reach to us too when we first realized the dimensions of the leap we had to make. From working with hundreds of people in recovery, we've seen at first hand the power of 12-Step programs in helping people stop destructive patterns of addiction. One feature stands out as supremely important in 12-Step programs: letting go of your own ego being in charge of your life and opening to the possibility of a Higher Power running the show. Making that move requires a leap across a metaphysical chasm worthy of an Indiana Jones movie.

In order to clear blame and criticism out of your body, you need to let go, at least for a moment, of your conviction that the other person has *anything to do with causing the thing you're blaming him or her for.* In other words, you must let go of thinking you're right, just as the alcoholic lets go of thinking he or she is in charge and doesn't have a problem. A moment's humble reflection is all most of us need to confirm how challenging that move really is.

We made that move hundreds if not thousands of times, catching ourselves starting to blame or criticize the other, then coming to a screeching halt in mid-thought or mid-sentence, wanting to halt the criticism but not knowing exactly what to do instead. Believe us, it took a lot of experimentation to answer the question "What do I do now?"

The Swap-Out

The only way to break the pattern of chronic blame and criticism is to institute a new habit of *conscious ownership.* When you feel the urge to criticize or blame the other person, for any issue whatsoever, you go to the opposite extreme: you *own* the issue yourself and release the other person from having anything to do with it. When you step into ownership, you actually reclaim the creativity you've been squandering in blame and criticism. It's as if you've had a major but invisible leak in your irrigation system that you repair so you can direct the flow by choice. You realize, *Oh,* this *is how I've been directing my creative juice unconsciously all this time. Now I choose to use it consciously in a new way.*

This bold move has awesome power to it. Ironically, many people think that letting go of being right puts them in a weaker position. It actually makes you stronger. By owning the situation, you claim full power over it. You also open the possibility of relationship magic by giving the other person the space to claim ownership also.

When we show couples how to do this, some get it right away, quick as a finger snap, while others struggle for months with breaking up the pattern of criticism. We found it equally difficult in our own early attempts, so we definitely feel compassion for anyone who takes up the awesome challenge of eliminating blame and criticism from their relationships.

What made it so difficult for us, and perhaps does for everyone, is that we were forced to swap out one entire metaphysical belief system for another. Both of us being stubbornly inclined, we made it very hard on ourselves. Imagine removing one program from your computer, a popular piece of software called "Look Everywhere All the Time for What's Not Working," and installing a new program called "Look Everywhere All the Time for What's Working Well." When you own the issue, new programs not only become apparent, they become usable, though the installation process may also involve learning new skills.

Both of us being stubbornly inclined, it took us several years of struggle and tough work to get the new program installed. There were no relationship manuals in those days; we had to find our way through by trial and error (with lots of emphasis on the "error" part!). One of our heroes, Buckminster Fuller, always said that he got to his wisdom by making every mistake he could possibly make. That's how we got our relationship wisdom too. Through all that trial and error, we found ways to keep you from making those mistakes and to heal the consequences of the ones you've already made. You're equipped with a guidebook we didn't have, so it's not likely to take you as long as it did for us.

Running Your New Software

Here's how you start to make the switch. Instead of the common blame-speak, such as "Why did you have to leave your socks on the floor for the hundred and eighteenth time?" you substitute a benign focus on your own role. It's important for your focus to be benign, though, because you cannot eliminate criticism by criticizing it or by exchanging criticism of your partner for self-criticism.

You entertain a new kind of thought in your mind, one that doesn't involve blame or criticism. You open up to wonder instead by thinking, *Hmmm, how could I make sure this never happens again?*

And you communicate this thought simply by saying, "I'm not sure what to do right now. I'm trying to figure out how to make sure this doesn't happen again."

Or you pause to consider another wonder question, one of the most powerful of all: *Hmmm, why am I having this particular issue at this particular time?*

Or you take an even bolder leap of ownership: *Hmmm, does this remind me of similar patterns in other relationships?*

By claiming ownership of the issue, you make a power shift in the relationship. In the past, you've thought of yourself as a victim of the person's behavior; now you step into the ownership position and, as a result, everything changes. One moment you're a passive participant in a drama of unfulfillment—just like sitting in a theater watching a movie you don't want to see. Even worse, you feel trapped inside the drama, unable to make it stop. The reason you can't stop it is because, without realizing it, your attention and participation are making the drama continue.

If you want to eliminate blame and criticism, there has to be a wake-up point, a moment when you choose to make the courageous step of owning the drama instead of claiming to be its victim. Using the theater analogy, there has to be a moment when you stand up, turn on the lights, and pull the plug on the projector.

It's the moment when you go from "Why are you doing this to me again?" to "I commit to doing whatever it takes to stop this pattern for good."

It's the moment when you catch yourself about to say, "Why are you picking on me again?" and swap it out for "I wonder why we always seem to get into fights on Friday evenings."

Rather than "You're trying to wreck our relationship," it's "I'm scared of losing you if things keep on this way."

You will find the Rule of Three Process in Appendix A helpful in identifying your unconscious patterns and making the shift into ownership. This is a good place to start if you are wondering where blame and criticism have been lurking.

Conscious Ownership Accesses Your Creative Wellspring

When you claim ownership of an issue, you simultaneously extend the opportunity for your partner to claim it. That's why we call it *conscious* ownership: the act of claiming responsibility for an issue simultaneously opens up room for others to own the issue too. Of course, that doesn't mean the other person is going to seize the opportunity and claim ownership—it simply opens up a possibility where none existed before.

When two people are locked in a struggle, they perpetuate the struggle as long as both are convinced they're the victims. In that scenario, there's no possibility of a breakthrough, because the power dynamics in the relationship are operating like a seesaw. One person goes up on the seesaw by saying, "It's your fault," then the other springs up with "No, it's yours." We've seen clear evidence that this pattern can be repeated, sometimes hourly, for decades. As one of our 40-ish clients put it, after hearing our seesaw analogy, "That's exactly what we've been doing for the past ten years. That's where our thirties went."

She was voicing a rueful truth, one shared by many people. Most people burn up their creative energy on the seesaw of Victim and Villain. For many of us, it's not just where "our 30s went," it's where our 40s, 50s, and 60s are going too. Taking a good, clear look at how you're spending your energy now—and whether any of it is being squandered unnecessarily through riding the Victim/ Villain seesaw—is a powerful step along the way to freedom and intimacy.

On the positive side, imagine the creative energy that is freed up the moment you get off the seesaw! In our own marriage we experienced a starburst of new creative energy when we kicked blame and criticism. With the new source of energy moving through us, we went on to write ten books together, raise kids, accumulate two million frequent flyer miles teaching seminars, and even survive the ultimate test of a marriage: remodeling a hundred-year-old Victorian.

Writing books or remodeling Victorians may not be your passions, but we're absolutely sure you've got powerful creative currents of your own stirring in you. Perhaps you haven't fully understood those passions and what you're going to do about them yet, but you very likely have not one or two but a treasure trove of creative ideas at work deep inside you. They're there for the beckoning, and the energy for accomplishing them is abundantly yours already.

All you need to do is stay off the seesaw. The energy expended in painful relationship drama is the exact energy you need to propel you along your accelerating creative path. In the next chapter you'll discover how to go to the core level of your deepest fears, so that you can rechannel the powerful energy of fear into excitement and creative zest.

Now, what can you do with all that free time and energy? We want to suggest growing your appreciation muscles. Since appreciation sparks connection and intimacy very quickly, you can notice your joy in each other's presence deepening on a daily level. To assist you in expanding your appreciation skills, we've included an appreciation interview, Customizing Your Appreciation, in Appendix A. The series of questions you use to tailor your appreciation to the receiver will heighten the effectiveness of your specially chosen communication and strengthen your blame-free zone.

CHAPTER SIX

From Fear to Flow with the Four Fear-Melters

Starting at midlife and accelerating thereafter, time seems to go by in a blur. Most of us feel an increased pressure to bring our personal lives and our relationship lives into harmony before time runs out. Unfortunately, most people respond to this pressure by sliding into despair or trying harder to do more of what already isn't working. The essential message of this chapter is that chronic problems—ones that recycle and never quite get resolved—are rooted in fear, usually hidden from both people in the relationship.

Here's the really good news: you can shift from fear to the flow of presence and spark of creativity quickly, easily, and reliably. In flow, you can choose new responses and deepen your intimacy. In fear, your partner looks like the enemy. In flow, he or she becomes your ally, your companion on the path. In fear, you must defend yourself from the perceived threat. In flow, threat dissolves into presence and contact. In fear, you don't see any possibility. In flow, solutions abound.

Fear fills the invisible fishbowl that most of us have been swimming in unconsciously for decades. It gradually permeates the moments of life, making us fear-logged and bogged down. Unnoticed fear reactions that distance us from our mates, such as cringing or holding our breath, gradually fade from awareness, leaving only the repetitive startles, freezes, faints, and fights echoing through the day. A lifted eyebrow, a certain tone of voice, the newspaper rattling, or the quick controlling reach create a coating of fear that gradually dulls presence and dampens creative connection in the moment.

In our culture, people don't typically name fear outright. Instead, they call it "anxiety" or "stress." Stress is simply long-term, habituated fear coursing through your nerves, muscles, blood, and organs. There are lots of statistics about the destructive results of stress, and they all point to long-held fear.

Whether you call it stress, anxiety, or just being uncomfortable, fear affects every aspect of your physical health. From your throat to your skin to your internal organs, your whole body reacts exponentially to the ongoing presence of fear. Your muscles tense, and over time this reaction can become chronic. You produce more blood flow to your muscles, up to 300 percent more, depriving skin and organs of the nutrients they need for ongoing health. Your adrenal system secretes increased amounts of cortisol, which cues your liver to produce more glucose, the blood sugar that feeds more fear responses. A host of cascading effects leaves you more at risk for cardiovascular and respiratory issues, including asthma and panic attacks. Your brain functioning suffers, as does your immune system. You may stop digesting food effectively, leading to other metabolic issues. And fear erodes emotional and relational well-being just as surely. You can't reach toward intimacy with loved ones from way back in your fear cave. From there, your beloved looks like the enemy. That's wired in; fear stops intimacy and fuels battles.

Fear contracts you so you cannot directly connect to, or sometimes even feel, the flow of your body's deep intelligence. You lose access to the wisdom of your community of 50 trillion cells, the circuitry that integrates your senses, feelings, and life experiences in a fraction of a second to support smart choices in your life.

As one of our clients said, "Fear makes you stupid." It's like a gradual hearing loss, except it's a fearing loss. Chronic anxiety can adversely affect the areas of the brain that control long- and short-term memory, as well as constantly activating your nervous system. Pervasive and habituated fear fuels prejudice, promotes labeling, and leads you to box your partner into a Not-Like-Me package you try to control or fix. When you lose connection through fear, you are much more likely to see the other as the source of what's wrong and drop into the conflict pit to duke it out.

Sophocles said something more than two thousand years ago that applies to everyone today: when you're scared, everything rustles. Your whole system gears up to react automatically when the rustle ripples through. Your blood moves toward your arm and leg muscles to ready for flight or attack. Your breath gets faster and higher, and the superaddictive hormone adrenaline floods your body. In the blink of an eye you're ready to slay the enemy, even though you've most often produced the enemy in your own head.

When we're in the grip of fear, we're hunkered down in the most ancient part of the brain, completely barricaded from the new kid on the block: the cognitive, reasonable cerebral cortex that can work things out. We go reptilian in fear, and Godzilla likes to smash things. And people like to smash Godzilla. Really, is this the sum of our human life on the planet—more and more ways to smash Godzilla?!

This leads to another big problem with fear in close relationships. We cannot talk ourselves out of fear! And our partners have even less success in telling us, "There's nothing to be scared of— just relax." *When you are scared, you don't have access to your logical brain.* Period. Think of the gates that drop with a loud boom in a security lockdown—that's your brain in fear.

If you look back at any destructive relationship interaction you've experienced, you'll find fear at the root. Unacknowledged, unexpressed fear runs conflict, power struggles, miscommunication, broken promises, and discarded dreams.

Here are some examples of how fear shows up in common relationship patterns:

- You criticize your mate, either out loud or in your mind.
- Your partner starts to look boring.

- You have things you withhold from your partner.

- You don't easily share your feelings when they arise.

- You imagine that your mate is hiding things from you.

- You experience regular bursts of disdain or contempt for your partner.

- You're not sure if you really love your mate as much as you did.

- You monitor your partner's activities and play Time Cop, Money Cop, or Sex Cop.

- You compare your mate negatively with others.

- You put a lot of time into improving your lover in some way.

Fear ultimately devolves into boring, tedious, dreary, and numbing interactions. First it gushes through your body with adrenaline, but the rush fades quickly and fatigue sets in. Then most people escalate the conflict so they can ride the roller coaster again. Subtlety disappears. Fear surges, as if you were YELLING AT YOURSELF AND YOUR PARTNER ALL THE TIME. Then conflict and power struggles become the norm, alternating with the despair and boredom of stressed-out bodies and repetitive arguments that go nowhere. "Here we go again" dims any possible bright horizon.

Fear Isn't a Big Deal—It's *the* Big Deal

Fear isn't just a big deal in intimate relationships—it's *the* big deal. When you face into fear and learn to turn fear to flow, you grow yourself, and you and your beloved grow together. When you don't, you grow further apart from your beloved and yourself.

Here's an even bigger problem in the culture: Many people believe that relationship would be boring without conflict and drama. They also believe that drama is inevitable. As we mentioned in the Introduction, a well-informed interviewer was rendered almost speechless recently when we told her we hadn't experienced any conflict in many years. She came back to the question at the end of the interview with a tone of "Oh, come on! Really?" and asked again, "You haven't said *anything* critical to each other in years? What do you talk about?" Indeed, what do you talk about? If you are convinced that drama provides the spark, you'll go for those adrenaline-laced interactions where blame and criticism escalate.

Adrenaline is a very powerful, extremely addictive hormone released with strong emotions—especially anger and fear—that concocts the blame and criticism cocktail we explored in detail in the previous chapter. People cannot be talked out of an adrenaline surge any more than they can get off the roller coaster once they're strapped in for the ride that gets its power from the drawn-out climb before the first big plunge. Amusement parks keep creating more and more extreme adrenaline rides, and so do relationship partners who don't realize they are addicted to the "gotcha" moment of being right. Adrenaline and fear tango together in an intimate dance that becomes dangerous to you and to your relationship's health.

People carry fear habits in their movements and gestures. Fear freezes, propels, collapses, or sprints people out of easy presence. Over time, movement habits develop into cringes, shrinking torsos, or jutting chests and chins. It's not hard to imagine what this might look like in a relationship conflict. Since criticism is the most common and destructive relationship habit, imagine partners who have been locked in mutual criticism for a while. Mike uses a combination of pointing, getting louder, and leaning into his wife's space. Lori dances with fear by shrinking into herself, holding her breath high in her body, and letting her sentences trail off as she darts her eyes back and forth, appearing to search for an escape route. This fear-based interaction has been escalating for some time, fueling an adrenaline rush for both Mike and Lori and then ending in more distance and despair. But it's been invisible to both of them as they've focused on the *words* they're using to criticize each other.

Making your point with words or scoring with logic doesn't budge fear—fear brushes past logic like a bull through a cobweb. You can be right and still be locked in fear, where nothing changes and intimacy seems more and more impossible. Until Mike and Lori learn to listen to their body wisdom and recognize their fear signatures, fear and adrenaline will continue to stoke their repetitive exchanges.

Paradoxically, the simplest fear signal—your breath—can also fuel your aliveness. Just as it does for other mammals, your breath slows or stops in the first instant of fear. The "huh" intake and holding of breath when startled or threatened is wired in and has been part of our physiology for thousands of years. The matrix of fear can't operate without the cooperation of your breath and the support of your movement—but these are also the gateways from fear to flow. When you shift your movements and restart your breath engine, you shift the deep fear reaction and open your ability to effectively respond here and now.

The Four Flavors of Fear

The four expressions of fear hold the keys to unlocking the powerful flow behind the dam. Most people recognize the phrase "fight or flight" but don't realize fear comes in four flavors that can also be blended into many combinations.

The **fear-fight** reaction often gets mistaken for anger. Imagine making fists, jutting your chin out, and barking, "Oh yeah, oh yeah!" as you thrust your body forward like a boxer. That in-your-face instant aggression most often masks fear, not anger. Fear-fight fuels blame and criticism, the reflexive attack that partners have learned to use to defend themselves.

The **fear-flee** reaction doesn't always involve dashing at high speed away from the threat. In modern times the tigers you're fleeing might take the shape of loved ones making demands on time or attention. Fear-flee looks and feels as if some of your awareness stays put in your body and some of you starts to leave. Imagine a shoulder moving away, or your head backing up, or your foot edging toward the door. Breath for fear-fleers diffuses and deflates like a pinhole puncture in a balloon. A fleer can disappear while his or her feet are still in the room. Relationship interactions caught in fear-flee often involve automatic nods and "uh huh's" instead of conscious listening. In extreme states of defense, fear-fleers make the "I'm out of here" move of literally heading out the door. They can threaten leaving to escalate the power struggle, which spikes adrenaline, taking the relationship on another roller-coaster plunge.

Our cat, Aliah, likes to be up high on her tower, overseeing the territory. Elevation is the best defensive position, which is also why forts have been historically built on the highest elevation in the surrounding area, and why homes on the hill are more expensive than those in the flatlands. Fear-flee can also move people toward the "high ground" when they're under attack, where they try to analyze fear away or "transcend" the issue by fleeing body sensations altogether.

Fear-freezing may be the easiest reaction to recognize. Just tighten your whole body while holding your breath. Imagine a loud noise and the startle that jolts your body. Or think of coming into a dark house at night and hearing a strange sound. Notice the whole-body halt that focuses your senses intently. That's fear-freeze. In relationships, fear-freezers often pair with fear-fighters. Imagine a hawk mating with a mouse and you can get a sense of the interplay between attack and freezing. One partner gets louder and in the other's face, or barks critical demands while the other freezes into invisibility until the storm passes. Each relationship partner brings a learned fear pattern into their current relationship that will repeat and escalate unless they shift into flow.

Many people overlook the **fear-faint**, but it has a powerful impact on our relationship interactions. Imagine your life energy draining out of your body through your feet, puddling beneath you. You might also experience a brain fog moment of "going stupid" that isn't actually an indication of intellectual decline but a fear signal. We've seen many relationships where one partner will get completely confused when the other gets loud and large.

Example:

Don: Where are the keys?! I gave them to you when we came in.

Lisa: I . . . uh, don't you have them? . . . You always keep them.

Don: Jeesh, can't you remember anything?!! That's why I. HAVE. TO. REMEMBER. EVERYTHING. Your mind is a sieve!

Lisa: Umm (swallowing and looking down), I'm pretty sure that, um . . .

Don: Oh, never mind. I'll find my spare set (stomps off).

Your favorite flavor of fear is a long-standing preference, since people bring their unresolved fears from the past into their current relationships, repeating their early adaptive strategies in the present in a patterned, unconscious way. For example, imagine a scenario where Dad often came home from work angry and frustrated and Mom tried to make him feel better. One of their children may have learned how to become invisible by freezing or fleeing so the wrath would land on someone else in the family. Another sibling may have found that a preemptive fighting strategy would distract Father long enough to make an escape. The invisible strategist formed a quiet, compliant temperament over time, whereas the fighter's aggression morphed into a rebellious attitude toward life. As adults, both are afraid of anger but have generated completely different, successful strategies for protecting themselves.

All the unloved fragments we bring to our partners—the anger about an old injustice or the sadness of a loss that hasn't been grieved—get cocooned in layers of fear. They may even seem to be the cause of yet more fear. Here are some of the most common forms emotional fear can take:

I'm afraid of my anger.
I'm afraid my sadness will go on forever.
I'm afraid of your anger.
I'm afraid of all my feelings, that I'll just run amuck.

When fear mixes with the primary emotions of anger and sadness, it creates some of the stickiest feelings that glue people in conflict and disharmony. Fear plus anger creates guilt. Fear plus sadness feels like an endless pit of despair. Fear plus judgment and anger feels like hot shame in your gut. Fear grips the other feelings and keeps them from opening into the free flow of energy and actual effective responding. But we've found that presencing fear starts to melt it away and open the gateway to authentic connection. When you experience fear melting, you open deeper feelings that can then be shared and explored.

Using the Fear-Melters to Move into Presence

So how can you recognize your fear signals and consciously shift into presence? What do you do if your partner continues haranguing or whimpering while you're doing your best to presence? Here's the good news. You can easily learn to discern your own fear signals and use simple movements to shift to flow. From flow you can grow into Full-Spectrum Presencing rather than the narrow lens of fear.

Our approach to fear works through shifting your body in reliable ways that open flow and allow you to access your cognitive brain and emotional brain rather than trapping you in the Godzilla realm where fear rules.

When you move your body in our Fear-Melters, you literally connect body to breath and breath to brain so you can respond creatively rather than react from a sense of perceived threat. The Fear-Melters provide an opening through which you can step into connection with your Full-Spectrum Presence and into resourceful choices.

These moves are deliberately simple to make them easy to access in the moments of defending. Here they are.

Fear-fighters can **ooze**. Imagine your hands and arms moving as if they were hot fudge over ice cream. Or let your shoulders, head, and spine undulate like seaweed in the gently rolling waves. Oozing melts the fight response, wakes up your whole-body breath, and dances you out of attack mode.

Here's an example of a couple integrating oozing into their daily lives:

> Erik and I have created a new play tool using oozing. When we begin to argue, we turn it into a slow-motion fight scene à la *Matrix* or *Batman*. We still get to express "fight" initially—which helps the shift/transition—but the slow motion adds fun and creative thinking, instills listening and responding, *and* gets our bodies oozing. Totally fun.

Meg, married more than 30 years, describes how oozing has changed long-held comparison and jealousy patterns with her husband:

> My competitor fight gal is so strong that she starts up when she hears the car door slam . . . before Tim has even walked through the door. So this is what happened with Tim when he returned from a weekend retreat.
>
> I heard the car door slam and his footsteps on the walkway. I could feel the fear rise up from my belly into my throat and I was leaning forward, and then I felt like an animal wanting to flee—looking for a hiding place. And even when my physical body was pulling back to show I wasn't scared, my energy was all forward in fight.
>
> So this time, I felt it coming on through my body and when he walked in the door, I said: "Hi, I'm going to turn the music on and ooze and move while you talk to me. Say anything you want, and I'll keep moving and oozing and listening. But don't talk to me for the next little while unless I'm oozing." So we moved and oozed together for at least 30 minutes while he told me what he'd been up to. At the end, I had created my own safety through oozing and my perception had widened to see a larger, safer landscape. Choosing to conduct a conversation while oozing greatly increased my feeling of being response-able.

Fear-fleers can **sumo**. They can spread legs wide and sink into the support of bent knees and solid pelvis. When a fleer places hands on thighs and gets down, feeling the floor, fleeing melts into full-frontal presence.

Harry, a single man in his 50s, describes how valuable sumo-ing has become to him:

> Fleeing has been a big part of my life's experience, from my first memories of running away at four years old to a recent flee when I noticed myself in midair after having unconsciously jumped out of the bed in the middle of an argument. That experience was my impetus to learn more about your work. Using sumo supports me in staying with the situation, and in combination with ooze, I slow down.
>
> When I notice my flee arise, which shows up as a physical spin around or sometimes as an inner spinning feeling, the first thing I do is name it to myself—I want to flee. Then I add breath as part of my sumo stance, imagining the weight of my breath going all through my body down to the ground and anchoring me. I imagine it as a sticky glue where I can move and place myself and stay connected. This has been very helpful to me. Yay! No more flee-fight slamming down the phone or leaving the room with a slammed door.

Fear-freezers are often told to "just relax," which is impossible in a frozen state. But freezers can **wiggle**. They can begin by wiggling fingers and/or toes and let the wiggling gradually expand to thaw out the frozenness in the rest of their bodies.

Here's a story one of our clients told us as an example of how the fear-freeze can be thawed in a relationship:

> Post-dinner, we decided to take a walk together (we have been prioritizing evening walks lately, noticing how simply taking the time to walk together generates so much more connection in our relationship). During the walk John casually asked me, "Hey, Linda, do you think you are in 'Freeze' right now? Is there something you are feeling afraid about? I notice you are walking, but you look rather frozen and I notice I don't feel connected to you." I paused, noticing I felt immediately defensive (a great indicator that he is probably spot on). In the moment, I didn't have any awareness of

feeling afraid. John then invited me to breathe and wiggle. I followed his suggestion, wiggling and shaking right there on the sidewalk. Using full-body breaths and wiggling, I was able to come back into presence, and soon enough I began to notice a tension in my jaw and shoulders. I was angry and I didn't even know it! My sense is that at some point during the day I had felt angry and then gotten afraid of my anger—thus, I went into freeze. I said out loud, "Mmmm . . . I feel angry." Each time I said this I felt myself come more fully into presence. John and I continued walking, exploring my anger with curiosity and feeling deeply connected as a result. What fun! Thank you, Fear-Melters!

Fear-fainters go all noodles-in-a-puddle and lose a sense of actually being in a body. They can **welcome** and give themselves **love scoops.** No part of us wants to be dismissed or killed off, and when fainters use their arms to reach out and embrace themselves, circling in to touch heart or belly, they come back home to right now and can choose consciously again.

Here's an example of using welcoming love scoops from one of our students who is single and a pastor:

I have noticed I've had strong attraction toward a wonderful man on our board. He has sensitive eyes, a brilliant smile, and gorgeous hair, and I've deeply appreciated his heart in his contributions to our discussions. I assumed he was married and so just enjoyed my own tingles and delights. I was approached by another pastor who wanted to set me up with him, and she asked if I was interested. My immediate response was a deflection. Oh, no, I can't, he's a member and on the board, etc. Pastors shouldn't date members, etc. I went to my office and realized I was afraid. I reached and gathered in, welcoming and scooping love especially to my heart area, and then felt that wasn't the whole of how I wanted to respond to her question. I returned to her office and presenced that I was really scared. I had stories—he was too handsome, I was too large, I'm not pretty enough, not his type, he wouldn't be interested. She was surprised, shared her perspective of me and more about him, and said she thought we would truly meet each other . . . She said for me to get over the too-big issue, and time to step into owning my own beauty. And asked again, "Would you like me to begin the conversation?"

Again with the welcoming love scoops Fear-Melter, I took several breaths and said yes. Two Sundays ago, I was preaching. I stepped into that big high pulpit, did my introduction of humor in church, and looked down to see him in the second row grinning from ear to ear.

Fear-Melters provide an opening, a breath of possibility that you can expand with new choices. Fear begets defensiveness, which hardens into withdrawal and contempt. The best result that can ever come from the fear cycle is the adrenaline burst and moment of successful defense. Then the cycle starts all over again. When you melt fear with these simple movements, you wake up new connections in your brain and new choices through your body. Follow a Fear-Melter with a few breaths and an appreciation, or a simple statement of something you notice in the moment, and you've presenced yourself and turned toward connection and intimacy.

These recycled relationship hassles don't dissolve until someone taps into and communicates the underlying fear. Communicating a simple "I'm scared" drops the armor and lets your partner know you are available to connect deeply. You're literally uncovering your soft parts to your mate, and that move disarms the reptilian brain and sparks the emotional, connecting brain.

Here's what this looked like in a Skype coaching session Katie led:

Teo and Adrienne have asked for assistance in determining whether they want to continue living together after a recent separation. As we explore their experience, I notice that Teo turns to look at Adrienne when she's speaking, but Adrienne only darts furtive glances at Teo when he is talking. I ask her to take a moment to exaggerate the darting glances, to make them bigger, and to notice what she experiences in her body when she does. She quickly realizes that she's afraid, and that her darting eyes are trying to flee. I ask her to drop into her legs and feel their solidness, a sumo move. After a moment the fear turns to flow as tears form in her eyes. She recounts her early experiences of keeping an eye on her stepdad, who would get abusive after drinking. As she shares, "I'm afraid to get close to you," both of their breathing deepens and their intimacy visibly expands.

Most fears dissolve into a deeper experience of aliveness with awareness and expression. However, the social masks that we are taught to wear obscure even the awareness of fear, much less its expression. So we wander off down analytical and historical paths when the simplest and most effective move is to say, "I'm scared." The expression might even be, "I'm scared, and I don't know why." The Fear-Melters are intended to connect all parts of your brain with the rest of your body so you can notice and you can express authentically. We're cultivating fear to flow to presence so you can be here. Here is where all the good stuff happens.

The Big Payoff for Moving from Fear to the Flow of Presence

We've been inspired by the enhanced intimacy that couples can celebrate when fear melts. Most partners don't realize how much their love has slowed to a trickle from long-held fear until their skin starts to glow, their eyes spark with renewed interest, and they are able to give and receive love again when fear drops away. Here's an example from a recent couples seminar where we were applying Fear-Melters to a recurring issue. Mark told us:

> When Rhonda's chin goes up in anger, I'm an immediate fleer—I'm out the door already. And what I noticed was that there was a softening that happened immediately, so when I went into sumo, first of all, I was immediately able to welcome what she said. Second of all, there was a difference because *she* was doing the melters too, and she was expressing herself differently, in a way that was *so* much easier for me to hear. So the whole thing changed, 'cause she changed as well.
>
> The pattern got completely interrupted. The pattern was, immediately running—run, duck, hide, cover. I was able to stop, I was able to get really present, then it was really easy to hear her.

Each partner can expand the direct experience of joy when fear releases to flow, as you'll hear in this exchange from Soorya and Jack. Soorya is speaking about a big shift in her flee pattern, and Jack's appreciation comes through at several points.

> I got something in a seminar about who I was. I was always complaining about how nobody saw me. I got that nobody could know how good and talented I was, or appreciate who I was. Then I saw that I was the kind of person who would run on the stage and shine for a moment, then run away and hide. So there was no one present whom they could applaud, because I'd left the stage really quickly to protect myself. I remember coming out with that, recognizing and claiming it, like, I started to feel that inner child coming back again. Then there was one time where I was encouraged by this counselor to run around and make the noise that I just couldn't make as a child . . . (Jack is making hmm-ing noises, and it sounds as though he hasn't heard this story and is very interested.)
>
> When I was running, and I could really feel my heart pumping, I was just alive again, and I remember saying, "The kid is back! The kid is back!" (Jack is laughing with delight as he says, "Beautiful, beautiful." Her delight ignites his, and they grin at each other.)

Remember that fear becomes a habit, and the fear filter makes your partner look like your enemy. In the middle of a battle, most people are unlikely to consider teaming up with the other side. So after Fear-Melters open flow, if you learn to shift into wonder and collaboration, you keep moving toward each other rather than away. You can learn to create possibilities to partner together toward what you really want. If you follow a Fear-Melter with a wonder question, you continue flowing toward harmony and co-creativity. You give your cognitive brain a better idea than how to inflict more damage. As a recent workshop participant noticed, "I'm realizing that lately fear is *way less* present in my thinking, so that leaves a lot more room for crazy, creative ideas."

Here are some wonder questions to try. Think of these as powerful pebbles to drop into the open pool that Fear-Melters provide:

Hmmm, I wonder how we can both have what we most want?
Hmmm, I wonder how we can easily resolve this issue?

Hmmm, I wonder how I can continue supporting you in expressing your deepest creativity?

Hmmm, I wonder what wants to emerge right now?

Hmmm, I wonder how I can express love in new ways?

Hmmm, I wonder how we can generate enough space for both of us to feel connected and fully engaged in our own creativity?

Hmmm, I wonder how I can most easily return to harmony and flow?

Releasing fear can open magic portals in your relationship where the formerly impossible becomes entirely imaginable. Michel explains his progression from fear to flow to co-creativity:

> For many years I had been dreaming and fearing about the idea of creating workshops for couples. Before meeting Josee, I kept judging myself as unstable and unable to facilitate workshops in this realm (even though part of me felt a *strong* pull toward this subject). Then we started reading *Conscious Loving* together and the initial spark came. We then enrolled in your introductory workshop. We both loved it and finally ended up taking the Couples Course. This workshop literally helped us discover how Fun and Play can unleash an incredible amount of energy/creativity while dissolving many fears. Through these exercises, I've learned *a lot* about Josee's inner world while finding "fun" strategies that contribute to some of her needs. It really brought me back to a place of playful energy that I've not felt since adolescence. Now that we have a *lot* more time having fun and laughing (instead of arguing), we are putting together a project in which we will facilitate outdoors weekends (trekking, kayaking) specifically designed for couples. We intend to help them develop a balance between their individual essence and their collaboration in fun and creative ways.

This may sound crazy, but consider this theory: most people are really scared to play. Playing fosters spontaneity, and spontaneity might foster some strange sound or movement that would be criticized or judged, and then you'd look stupid, strange, weird, or silly. Looking silly terrifies people more than being stuck forever. Humans have endured millennia of competition for resources and mates, and being too different could result in a death sentence.

The truly different ones became the shamans or wandered off from the tribe to forge their own adventures or got shunned. Shunning, being ignored and turned away from, meant death. Modern humans carry those genetic memories and still react strongly to the opinions of others. In many modern communities, bullying has replaced shunning, but the message is the same: be like us or die. Not the most germane soil to cultivate play. As Kathy, one of our colleagues in a 25-year-plus same-sex relationship put it, "In the Eastern European tradition from which I come, you suffer and then you die. I was truly shocked to discover that basic happiness was okay, a worthy goal to have. For real, I didn't buy the whole love business. You get to have this really good couple of years, good sex, then it falls apart. The great gift from conscious loving was the releasing of the 'should.' You should have this job, you should make this much money, you should visit each other's family (radical and revolutionary to learn I could make my own choices about visiting or not visiting). Now we play at a level that I wouldn't have imagined—squirt gun fights, persona parties, making up roles with each other." Julie, Kathy's partner, adds, "The context of our relationship is, what's the next magic?"

In our close relationships, we can create the freedom to play with each other. The most challenging moments for our clients and students in seminars involve stepping from fear-driven seriousness ("working on the problem") to flow-driven connection, contact, and spontaneous play. When partners play, they quickly erase the conflict and return to harmony.

For example, listen to Donna sharing an interchange with her partner, Diana:

> After completing the Couples Course in Toronto last year, Diana and I celebrated by going out to dinner. We found a lovely restaurant, had a fab meal and great conversation. Just before the bill came, something came up and we got stuck in an old pattern of blame/not feeling understood. We walked back to the hotel room in silence, a bit in shock that things had derailed so quickly. When we entered our room, I picked up the soft ball we had been given in the course and tossed it to Diana, asking her to tell me more about what she

was feeling about what I had said while tossing the ball back and forth *and* making funny faces. She started and only got about six words out when we both collapsed on the floor laughing. That was the end of the issue. It evaporated and we never discussed it. What had seemed so real was clearly us ulping [shorthand for "Upper Limit Problem"] ourselves out of a happy, expanded state.

It's been said that play is the highest form of research. As you loosen the grip of fear, your partnership evolves into a wide-open field for play and discovery, and this field continues to deepen and expand the more you play. Eventually you move from working through issues to playing through them. It took us a few years to get to that play space, but once we discovered it we sure wanted to spend more time there. We predict you will too. The best thing about play is that it's always available to you. Next time you feel a wave of anxiety or fear, use one of the Fear-Melters to play your way through it instead of carrying around fear's unpleasant symptoms in your body.

CHAPTER SEVEN

Facing Death and Loss in Relationships

From midlife onward into older age, our relationships are touched more each day by death and loss. How do our minds make sense of this—especially when death and loss often visit us in such unthinkable ways? We're still wondering and learning from a shocking loss in our own lives several years ago. A 60-ish colleague of ours, recently remarried, undertook a yearlong project of building a dream house. On the day it was complete, he invited friends to visit for a housewarming. The house was a work of art, breathtaking in its detail; our colleague and his wife were showered with compliments on their taste and perseverance through the expensive rigors of the project. When we waved good-bye to him, there was dance music pumping through the house and a party going on. The next day he drove out to a beautiful spot where he loved to hike and shot himself in the head.

How do you make sense of an event like that? In our experience, you don't. But we need to admit the reality of death into our relationships, for one fundamental reason: how we are with death is how we are with life. To shrink from one is to shrink from the other. The same is true for matters of the heart: how we are with death is also how we are with love.

Pressure mounts after midlife to embrace the wholeness of life. The *Tao Te Ching,* the ancient Chinese book of wisdom, says, "The surest test of your sanity is whether you can accept life whole, as it is." Embracing the reality of death and welcoming it into the wholeness of your self is a gateway to a richer, deeper experience of love with your intimate beloved.

Facing Death: What an Exhilarating Position to Be In!

If you're over 45 you are in a time of your life when you can become exceptionally richer in love. At midlife a stark awareness grows on us: I have a dwindling number of days to live my life. Then, to turn up the volume on this awareness, we often have a near miss of some kind. All it takes is a health scare or a close encounter with a city bus to make us realize that we may have been overly optimistic when we estimated our dwindling amount of life in days. It might be seconds.

When this awareness finally hits home, some people respond to it by plunging into despair. They give up on their dreams and busy themselves with distractions. Maybe you've felt that kind of despair in the past—both of us have had our moments of it too. But you're not like that anymore. If you're reading this book you're one of those who take up the challenge. You're taking the essential steps in your campaign to make the second half of life the best half. That's what we chose to do, and it's what we want you to do.

How can we face death and loss in a brand-new, and even exhilarating, way? A woman, the longtime student of a Zen teacher, was dying of cancer. In her final hours, the woman's teacher came to visit her bedside. At one point the teacher leaned over and whispered something that made the dying woman laugh out loud, a sound the other mourners in the room had not heard for a long time. After the teacher left, the others wanted to know what the teacher said that made the dying woman laugh. What the teacher said was, "Don't pretend for a moment that you're not dying!"

If that immediacy and full-out living is what you want too, take a deep breath and open the gateway to adventure by realizing this:

Your days, like ours, are numbered.

Whether they're numbered in years, days, or seconds is one of life's great and maddening mysteries—an elusive elf of a problem that's always disappearing just around the corner of what our minds can conceive. Until science perfects a test that can give us the day and hour of our expiration date, we're content to let the moment of our ultimate departure rest in the realm of magic and mystery. There are much more important things to focus on.

What We Know About Loss

At midlife and beyond we all live inside two concentric circles of expanding awareness. One circle is what we know about ourselves and the world. You're more experienced now in so many areas than you were at 20 or even 40. As you grow into your 50s and onward, you have a hard-won and refined sense of the person you are. You have a better sense of how the world works, and you're using yourself more fully and creating with breadth, depth, and impact.

At the same time, though, you're living inside another expanding circle of awareness. You're becoming more aware by the day of the mysteries of life—all the things you don't know, plus all the things you don't even know you don't know. For example, if any of us had been alive a thousand years ago, we would probably have thought the earth was flat . . . if we thought about it at all. We can assume that there's as much or more about the world we don't know today, and no doubt an even vaster store of things we don't know we don't know.

To develop ourselves fully in the second half of life, we need to balance our pride in what we know with a genuine awe for the mysteries of what we don't know. We've seen all too many people slide into thinking, as they move past midlife, that they have everything all figured out. Long before we became therapists, we had many opportunities to interact with folks like that in our own families. Perhaps you did too. We're very familiar with the hazards of this kind of premature "hardening of the categories." It can lead in later life to bitter recrimination about lost potential and a "you kids get off my lawn!" approach to social interactions.

We know a lot more about loss now than we did 35 years ago when we first met. Some of it we learned by dealing with it up close in our own lives, some of it we learned from helping clients deal with losses in their lives. In sharing what we know about death and loss, we also want to maintain a healthy respect for the unknown, what remains to be discovered as you allow the concentric circles of your awareness to expand.

Loss is loss, no matter whether we lose a family member, a beloved pet, or a job we depend on. Loss can occur anytime and anywhere we invest our hearts. Loss must be respected as a natural force of life, just like an ocean wave. When loss comes upon us, though, the human tendency is to pull away from its reality.

Gay remembers that as a child growing up in Florida, he was told not to turn his back to the waves when playing in the ocean. It's useful advice, no matter what kind of wave you're dealing with. We've worked with many people who tried to turn their backs on waves of loss. They distracted themselves from feeling their deep grief by getting busy, getting drunk or stoned, getting into another relationship right away, and any number of other attempts to make reality go away.

The first thing we must do when death or another form of loss visits us is often the hardest: to open ourselves to all our feelings—anger (the hard one), fear about what's next, sadness about what might have been, leftover recriminations.

No matter how much support from others you have or don't have, the journey through grief is ultimately a solo expedition. Presencing becomes an invaluable skill to fully experience loss. You need to get to the center of your grief and feel it. As you do so, you perform a benign act of nuclear fission in your creative life. By allowing yourself to feel the full dimensions of your grief and the complicated mix of feelings that come along with it, you also open the gateway full and wide to your creativity. By surrendering yourself, by letting yourself feel the full depths and heights of all your emotions—in other words, by letting yourself go into the unpredictable unknown of your feelings—you catapult yourself into the wildness of your creativity, into the exhilaration of the next creative possibilities.

Grief Comes in Waves and Defies Time

Grief comes in waves, often with days, months, or years between waves. That's another reason it's so important to honor grief as the powerful force it is. We've seen many people get into a new relationship quickly while they still had waves of grief to handle from a past one. This doesn't mean we all need to wait years between relationships, just that we need to be sensitive to the appearance of old grief while we're trying to find new love.

We are often asked how long it takes to recover from loss, whether it's loss by the death of a partner or through less final means such as a breakup. We can give you an estimate based on what we've seen, but like almost everything else in the human sphere, it has a lot of variability in it. Based on being with several hundred people who have lost partners through death, we can say it takes one to two months for every year of the relationship to heal from loss. In other words, if you lose your partner of ten years through death, give yourself 10 to 20 months to move through the major after-waves of your loss. In reality, you'll have mini-waves of grief and thoughts of the lost partner for many years, perhaps always. Your ability to embrace rather than shun those thoughts and feelings is the true measure of your healing from the loss.

Often when people ask the question of how long it takes, what they're really asking is "Why haven't I been able to move through my grief and get on with my life?" They feel a pull to move forward into something new, but they feel a stronger pull from the past. The result: a state of inertia that can easily drag into depression.

We've worked with many people who have gone far beyond the "one to two months for every year" estimate. In fact, we've worked with people whose partners died a decade or more ago but who have not yet moved through the grief. The old sayings tell us that "time is the great healer" and "time heals all things," but as one of our clients, a remarkable woman we'll call Beth, put it, "Time is taking its own sweet time about it."

Beth came to us at age 50 after losing her husband of many years to cancer. Six years after her husband's death, she still felt unable to move past her loss. Her decision to visit us was inspired by panic and a two-week bout with back pain that she suspected was related; finally, a man she found attractive was asking her out on dates. She hadn't been able to bring herself to say yes. She could feel the pull in her body and mind between the urgency of her desire for a new future and the burden of grief she was still carrying.

A Body-Mind Paradigm for Healing Grief

Beth was ripe for a new paradigm. Her old paradigm was rapidly running out of fuel, no matter how hard she stomped on the accelerator. It was making last-gasp sputters she could feel in her body, a constant swarm of butterflies that seemed to inhabit her belly.

Beth's existing paradigm for healing her grief came largely from her religious background. She and her husband were devoted to their church; when he died at the age of 46 she was surrounded by a loving and attentive community who attempted to help her the best way they knew how. The comforts of their paradigm at first gave her some peace. She said, though, that after a while "I got so tired of hearing 'he's in a better place now' that I wanted to scream. It seemed like every message I got was the same thing, 'Sure, you're sad now but you don't really need to be because he's in a better place.'"

Beth found this form of comfort ultimately stultifying, and the reason for her dissatisfaction gets to the heart of why she needed a new paradigm for healing grief. What Beth resented most was that the old paradigm attempted to talk her out of her feelings, whatever they were. If she got too sad she should comfort herself with the idea of her husband being in a "better place." If she got scared she could rely on the help of the community to get her back on her feet. That is, assuming she stayed within the limits of the rules, and that's where Beth's journey to the center of her grief really began.

Her former community's well-meaning attempt to lift her out of her grief also took her away from the authentic feelings in her body. The body is where we feel the pain of missing someone and the ache of loneliness. By offering a mental concept to Beth—"picture your husband in heaven instead of focusing on his death"—her community was doing the best it knew how to help her get free of the grip of the pain in her body.

However, the use of mental pictures to escape emotional pain in our bodies is only a short-term fix, the same essential procedure that hypnotists use to put people in trances and stick pins in their arms without causing a flinch. It only works as long as the trance lasts.

When Beth tried to talk about some of her feelings—anger in particular—she found that members of her community did not listen generously. When she raised big questions about whether there was anything like an afterlife or a heaven, she got met with stony looks or with pats on the back reassuring her that she would soon be over it.

Beth ultimately bolted from the community and struck out on her own to find a new life, where she read one of our books and found her way to us. When we met her she was six years away from her husband's passing and a year into her new life out west. However, even though she tried to put two thousand miles between her and the old paradigm, it had followed her all the way across the country.

Now she was feeling the limitation and pinch of it more than ever, because she was being offered the opportunity to date a man she felt attracted to. It was the first time in six years she'd felt like saying yes, but she could also feel a strong pull in her body to tuck back inside and say no. New feelings were awakening in her, and they were scaring the heck out of her.

Beth needed to break free from the trance of all her mental concepts about death. She needed a new paradigm, one that took her deeply into the authentic feelings in her body rather than away from them. Instead of going up into her mind to console herself with pictures of heaven, she needed to learn how to plunge herself into the center of her grief and come out whole on the other side. The way out of grief, we told her, is always *through*.

As for social life, we suggested to her, "Surround yourself with people who will talk you *into* your feelings rather than out of them." In other words, be with people who give you room to feel what you actually feel and listen nonjudgmentally to you. We modeled that for her by telling her that she was free to explore any and all feelings, especially the ones she'd never told anybody about.

And reveal she did. Beth made the courageous decision to remove the buffer of her mental concepts and confront directly the raw and authentic emotion her body still held from her husband's death. The big one was anger. Anger was a challenge for Beth to let herself feel, as it is for many people, because her husband had been a good man whom she loved very much. Members of her community called him a "saint." However, she also carried a big load of unexpressed anger that she felt guilty about even having.

Those complex feelings confused Beth and caused so much cognitive dissonance in her that she kept them hidden from others. She was even successful for many years at hiding them from herself. Fortunately, our bodies and minds do not like that solution very much, and usually devise some way to reveal important feelings to us. For Beth, it was the two-week bout with back pain that finally woke her up to the need for urgent change.

According to John Sarno, M.D., the legendary back pain specialist who treated thousands of patients at New York University's Rusk Institute of Medicine, most back pain is caused by muscle tension from unacknowledged and unexpressed anger. Dr. Sarno found that only a tiny percentage of back pain, less than 10 percent, was actually caused by a problem that could be improved by surgery or pharmaceuticals. His prescription for 90 percent of back pain sufferers was simple: learn how to feel and express your anger and your back pain will go away. It turned out to be true for Beth. Her back pain disappeared once she contacted and brought forth the things she was angry about.

That first day we met with her, the air in our office was almost electric. Beth for the first time in six years voiced her anger at her dead husband. One thing she was profoundly angry about was that they'd tried for years to get pregnant, finally deciding to adopt two babies from a faraway continent. They spent a year going through the complications of the adoption process, but then amidst the joy and tumult of having two new infants to take care of, her husband got sick and went into his decline. Instead of the joy she had expected, her first year with the babies was a frantic blur of sorrow, frustration, and fatigue followed by heartbreak: her husband died a month before he could see the girls take their first steps.

We could see the change come over her face as Beth told us about that and other anger she'd accumulated. Her brow let go of a host of worry wrinkles; the hard set of her jaw eased. There was more, though: if anger was hard for Beth to confront, the fear beneath the anger was even harder.

For many of us, talking directly and honestly about our fear is even more challenging than talking about anger. The same is sometimes true of sadness. We've had many clients tell us they were unable to let themselves let go enough to cry about the loss for months, even years, afterward. A breakthrough moment in that first session with Beth came when she got underneath her anger and spoke about her fear.

We asked her to make a presencing move, to tell us how she experienced fear in her body. She pointed to her stomach and said,

"I think I'm scared practically all the time." And who wouldn't be? Here are some of the things she told us she was scared about. Wherever you are in your life and whatever your experience has been, take a moment to put yourself in Beth's situation:

- You're a woman about to turn 50, with two children starting first grade.

- You quit a good job 20 years ago to become a full-time wife and support person for your husband's career. You have no idea if you can retool yourself to make it in the current work environment. Perhaps worse, you're not even sure you want to go back to work. You've already got a full-time job raising two kids, and you've also got creative dreams you've been thinking about for years. You've got an idea for a little business you want to start. It scares you, but it also excites you and engages your passions.

- Now a man you like is asking you out, but after everything you've been through, you are terrified by the prospect of having to take care of one more person.

Loosening the Grip of Limiting Beliefs

Here's where a pivot point occurred, a moment when Beth's life took a big swerve to the positive. To understand its importance a brief explanation is called for. One thing therapists are trained to listen for is when a client expresses a limiting belief. A limiting belief is a personal rule you're unconsciously operating out of, a rule that's true for you but not for everybody else. For example, "You simply cannot trust a man/woman" is a limiting belief you might hear a discouraged person say in the wake of some betrayal of the heart.

A limiting belief is when you say something you unconsciously believe to be true that's not actually true, a personal rule that limits your possibilities. Look at the example of Gay's Uncle Bob and Aunt Audrey, who moved next door when he was ten years old:

I would sometimes stop to chat with Uncle Bob, who would often be sitting on his back steps, whittling or working crossword puzzles. I soon discovered that he was usually out there to escape the confines of the house, recovering from one of his frequent battles with my Aunt Audrey. Audrey was a retired chief of staff for a U.S. senator; she was an Iron Lady when Margaret Thatcher was but a clever girl in pigtails. For 40 years she had worked on Capitol Hill, shaping policy and telling an office full of people what to do every day.

Now, though, most of her policy initiatives revolved around cataloging the many urgently needed improvements in Uncle Bob. He was the only person except the gardener she got to boss around. The long-suffering gardener, whom I'd see with his head bowed for long periods of time listening to Aunt Audrey, only came once a week.

One time I came across Uncle Bob sitting on the back step, and in the course of our conversation he said something I didn't know at the time was an "old saying." He sighed and said, "Women. You can't live with them and you can't live without them." Being one of those relentlessly curious kids who were always asking, "Why?" I asked Uncle Bob why you couldn't live with women or without them. He said, "You can't live with them because you can't ever please them. They're just naturally dissatisfied all the time. That's the way they are."

I asked him why you couldn't live without them—at ten years old it seemed to me like a pretty good solution—but Uncle Bob said he'd have to explain that one to me later. He never did, though, as you will soon see, because that was our last back-steps conversation. Before administering the punch line of my final chat about relationships with Uncle Bob, let me highlight the key point: Uncle Bob was operating out of a limiting belief. In the universe at large, there are probably hundreds of millions of women who can be pleased and who go around feeling satisfied with their husbands and life in general. In the universe of Uncle Bob, such women did not exist. He had a limiting belief that excluded the possibility of women being pleased and satisfied around him. Knowing Aunt Audrey as I did, I could see his point. I don't think I'd ever heard her say anything remotely positive about Uncle Bob. But at the same time I was aware, even at a young age, that Uncle Bob's situation didn't necessarily apply to anybody else.

The truly memorable moment in the conversation, the one that's still rattling around in Gay's head 50-some years down the line, came when an innocent question popped into his mind, which he made the mistake of asking: "Why do you think you picked Aunt Audrey, then? She doesn't seem all that easy to please." Oops, end of conversation. Uncle Bob got up and took his crossword puzzles elsewhere.

Beth's Limiting Belief

Beth's limiting belief was a great deal subtler than Uncle Bob's almost comic-book version, but it was built of the same components. You can spot Beth's limiting belief in that last fear she expressed: a man she likes is asking her out, but after everything she's been through, she is terrified by the prospect of having to take care of one more person. Her limiting belief is that being in a relationship with a man *automatically* means she will be put in a caretaking role. There's no question she came by this belief the hard way, by many years of sacrificing her own wants, needs, and dreams in the service of caretaking, but now the belief was coming to the surface to be evaluated. Life itself was knocking on the door, asking her the question, "Would you be willing to let go of caretaking and create a completely new kind of relationship with a man?"

We asked her to take a step into the present and embrace that question directly. "Take a moment right now to imagine a loving relationship with a man where caretaking is absolutely not an issue. Imagine a relationship where it's about how much love you can give and receive, where maybe even he enjoys taking great care of you! Feel how being in a loving relationship with a man could be about freedom and ease instead of any kind of burden."

Beth's eyes practically crossed at that point. "How does that work?" she asked.

"There's only one way we know of. You just choose to make it up from scratch. You make a conscious choice to open up to the possibility that you can create something brand new. You don't need to repeat the past if you let yourself learn from it. And one of the best things you can learn is that you can dream up a new kind of relationship, one that's free of the past. Are you willing to do that with us right now?"

She took about ten seconds to let the ramifications of our question settle in her body and then said, "Yes." Her new life began in that choice.

What if she hadn't been ready yet to say yes? Grief has no timetable carved in stone, so even after six years it still might not feel like the right time for Beth to start anew. In our view, a sincere no is just as meaningful as a sincere yes. The yes meant she was ready to move forward, but if she'd said no, it would certainly have been understandable. We knew, from helping thousands of single people manifest new love in their lives, that you need to feel down deep "in your bones" that *now* is the right time to set the forces of attraction in motion that will bring a new mate to you.

Creating a New Now

We saw Beth half a dozen more times over several months, assisting her in getting through the numerous glitches and celebrating the minor victories of welcoming the new man into her life. We were pleased when she told us that the new man liked to give her foot massages and bring her cups of tea in the evening. Plus, he was a little older than Beth and had raised two children of his own; he was in a phase of his life when he really enjoyed reading the good old bedtime stories to her young ones.

If you are reading these words, you may be one of those many millions of people all over the world who are in the grip of loss. It could be an ancient loss, such a heavy assault on your heart that you've never fully recovered from it. It could be a loss that's closer to right now, today. Whether close or far away in time, the loss still feels real to you. There is nothing wrong or abnormal about the echoes of ancient pain—the big losses can tug at our hearts across decades.

If those words speak to you, here's what to do: Follow Beth's inspiration, step by step. Stand free in the present moment and ask yourself the crucial question, "Am I willing to complete the past and create a brand-new kind of relationship in my life now?"

Listen for a sincere yes or a sincere no: both are equally valuable. Find out if this is the moment for you to start anew. You don't need to know how. In fact, not knowing how is essential to the process; it means you're standing in the present moment, simply owning the space of your sincere yes or no.

What if you can't get a clear yes or no? That actually happens quite often; after all, most of us don't get much training in listening to our intuitions or the deeper communication from our innermost being. If you don't get a clear choice on the line right away, come back to the question later and circulate it through your mind later. There's no statute of limitations on when liberating insights come; often they drop in when you're doing other things, such as dreaming, taking a bath, or sweating at the gym.

We've included a simple yet powerful process in Appendix A to move through loss and locate yourself in the present possibilities and connections in your life. This tool focuses on a specific aspect of presencing that allows you to release the past and use your whole-body wisdom to stand in the now. Thousands of people have found Unhooking the Source of immediate value as they move through change and loss and face the only place where life happens, the exhilarating now.

Loss is something that happens to every one of us, tall or short, rich or poor, four-star general or part-time cabbie. Wherever we are in life, we are never far from loss. It is unsettling for most of us when we first confront the pervasiveness of loss in our world. Ultimately, though, we can take great comfort from knowing we're all in it together.

Until our minds can someday comprehend the full mysteries of existence and nonexistence, our hearts must continue to do the big work. The big work of loss is to accept it and all your feelings about it thoroughly, so that unembraced elements of it don't keep you impoverished in love long afterward. This is a major task, and unfortunately nobody can do it for us. However, there is a sweet reward for doing the big work, for allowing yourself to feel the immensity of loss, for consciously acknowledging even the bitter aspects of it. The reward is that through your struggles to embrace all the feelings loss brings with it, you open up a big, new space of compassion in yourself. This new sense of self-acceptance becomes a wellspring you can draw on and offer as a gift to others.

Compassion is one of the finest feelings available to humans, in our experience. There's no human experience we've seen that isn't enhanced by compassion. Yet authentic compassion is also quite rare in our experience. Take a moment now to savor this rare, fine experience by opening your heart to yourself once again, accepting all the losses of your life and the feelings that go along with them. Then, as you go about in the world, notice how more compassion for yourself naturally opens up a greater resonance with and acceptance of other people.

CHAPTER EIGHT

Two Ten-Minute Conversations a Week

Most couples suffer from a lack of intimacy—but the loss often goes undetected because it erodes so slowly they don't notice it. Here's why: Emotionally rich communication gets extinguished over time, replaced by random talk about the "stuff" of life—a child's dental appointment, the broken upstairs toilet, who's going to pick up food after work. Communication about "stuff," particularly about "stuff that's not working," gradually becomes the dominant tone of the relationship.

One of the best things we ever did in the early years of our own relationship was to come up with a new solution to that problem. We put it to work first in our own lives, in the form of two sit-down conversations per week, each devoted to a specific purpose. We devoted one ten-minute session to what we designated Stuff Talk, all the business-y things that need to be dealt with in every relationship. We devoted the second sit-down conversation to what we called Heart Talk: all the feelings, both tough and tender, that often don't get discussed consciously in the course of the week.

Our own Heart Talks and Stuff Talks were much longer in the beginning, usually a half hour or more. As we began to teach other couples how to do the process, though, we found that briefer is better. We discovered that thinking of it as a ten-minute process rather than an open-ended one made it work better, partly because there was a clock ticking in the background. Shorter meetings were also helpful in getting cooperation from both partners (especially if one of those partners happened to be a man!). We were pleased to discover over time that most couples can easily do the Heart Talk and the Stuff Talk in less than ten minutes.

We'll have more to say about that shortly, but first, explore an important question with us.

What Does It Really Take to Solve a Problem So It Doesn't Return?

Most relationship problems never really get solved. They return again and again, sometimes on a seemingly perpetual tape loop. All too often, they resurface across time and space in different relationships. By midlife, most of us have solved the relationship problems we know how to solve. What's left to confront are the crystallized issues we don't know how to get our heads or hearts around.

While that can be a maddening feature of relationships at midlife and beyond, it actually has a powerfully positive possibility built into it. When we work with a couple or a single person, we always start by asking them what the absolute most important outcome would be, a life change that would make them say something like, "Wow, I can hardly believe it, but I actually made *that* happen!"

In other words, we're looking for what would make the biggest difference to them first. In working with relationships after midlife, we've found that there are usually only one or two problems that have eluded earlier attempts to resolve them. However, those one or two problems are often so entrenched by midlife that only a radical procedure can release them. Although the instructions are simple for both the Ten-Minute Stuff Talk and the Ten-Minute Heart Talk, both are radical procedures—they go to the root of the problem and set in motion its release.

There's another major reason problems often never get resolved, another force that causes them to linger and recycle for years: Many people, when they really get in touch with themselves, realize they were never actually committed to solving the problem. In fact, many people discover that far from being committed to solving the problem, they were unconsciously committed to keeping it going. In other words, they didn't realize they had an unconscious commitment to perpetuating the problem that was bigger than their conscious intention to solve it.

What would cause such a thing? Why would people—often extremely smart and good-hearted people—go out of their way to keep from solving a problem . . . often for decades? The main reason we found is that there is a larger and more painful issue that would need to be confronted if the problem were actually resolved. Not solving the problem keeps the bigger issue at bay. For example, if a couple can keep fighting, year in and year out, about socks being left on the floor, they can distract themselves from asking whether they are each fulfilling their own creative destiny.

However, it's hard to avoid the big issues forever. No amount of distraction can ultimately quell the gnawing awareness that our creative potential is being squandered. It is a special kind of pain; it feels deeper than the physical, more down near the soul. It's the growing sense that we won't get to make our unique and singular contribution. Around the world, whether you're looking into the eyes of a beggar in Calcutta or a wealthy socialite in Beverly Hills, you recognize the pain caused by lack of creative fulfillment.

When we work with a couple or a single person, our goal is to help them end that pain as soon as humanly possible. To end the pain requires a radical adjustment, something that can break up the cycle of repetitive conflict that never quite gets resolved. What's needed is something that can halt the destructive pattern and clear the path for some brand-new conscious choices that partners can reliably use in the day-to-day life they create together. There's only one thing we've found that's powerful enough to cause that kind of transformation.

Conscious Commitment

We've been privileged to see a certain look of astonishment on the faces of many people as they made a breakthrough—suddenly realizing they had the power of choice. One moment they were thinking of themselves as victims of a lot of bad breaks, then a new possibility dawned: *I actually got here through a series of* choices, *most of which were so totally unconscious they didn't even seem like choices!*

To wake up to the power of choice is to seize control of your life from the forces of your unconscious—the part of you that compels you to fret, blame, and procrastinate. The moment you celebrate the power of choice—*Wow! I make up my life one choice at a time!*—you also pull the plug on your old unconscious programming. The roiling, restless ferment that's been driving your dissatisfaction suddenly turns into a reservoir of creative energy. You have a new energy source to draw upon.

Being with people as they make those realizations is one of life's best experiences; even though we've seen it dawn on people many times, it always comes like a beautiful sunrise. No matter how many gorgeous sunrises we've seen, the next one inspires just the same awe.

Committing Leads to Conscious Choosing

Choosing comes to its full fruition in the act of committing. It's one thing to say to a potential marital partner, "You're the one I want." Making that choice is a key step, but the real magic happens when you go all the way with your choice. When you stand before a religious authority or a judge at your wedding, the assembled multitude—whether it's a multitude of a thousand or a few—isn't there to see you point to your beloved and say, "You're the one I want." They're not going to go home happy until the moment they hear you say something definitive, such as "Yes, I do." Some members of the multitude are probably waiting to hear an authority figure say, "I now pronounce you married" and see a signed document that has your name on it.

A couple came in a while back with an unusual problem. After 14 years of living together harmoniously, through illness and health, hard times and good times, Jerry and Jen had finally decided to get married. The day after the wedding they got into an argument the likes of which they had never seen in all their years together. Their relationship fell apart; after years of contentment living together, within three weeks of their wedding they weren't speaking.

What could possibly account for such a thing? Jerry and Jen eventually got their flow going again, but not until they understood the force they'd unleashed. You turn on one of the most powerful forces in the universe by uttering the magic word "Yes" (or in this case, "I do"). An even more powerful force gets set in motion when you speak your "Yes" in public and accompany it with a signed document. That's the kind of yes that sends your life off in a different direction.

We all create our world through the power of yes and no. The choices we make send us in one direction or another. Yes creates one world. No creates an entirely different one. We can tell you, though, from 30-plus trips around the world teaching relationship seminars, that many of us are not aware of the power of choice.

For example, through repeated unresolved conflict, many people become entrenched in thinking of themselves as victims and the other person(s) as villains. If the perception of oneself as a victim goes on long enough, it can obscure a fact that is dazzlingly obvious usually to everyone else: *I got to where I am through a succession of choices.*

In teaching seminars, we've seen a certain stunned look on many people's faces when this awareness sinks in:

Wow, you're right! It was my choice *to go out with him/her!*

Wow, you're right! It was my choice *to invest in my brother-in-law's gold mine!*

There is great liberation in realizing the power of choice. With one swoop you free yourself from the bondage of the victim position; that by itself would be a fine outcome. However, at the same time you also unleash one of the world's greatest untapped resources in your favor. Few people realize they are creating their lives by moments of choice. Once you awaken to this realization, you occupy a rarified territory in the stratosphere, a zone where you and other awakened people are literally creating magic by making simple, easy choices each day that make radical, positive changes in your relationships.

By living your new life out of this awareness—that you are creating your life one choice at a time—you have an awesome power at your fingertips in every moment. Your only question is: *What do I want to do with this power?*

That was the position we found ourselves in when we woke up to this realization a year or two into our marriage. One of the best inventions that emerged from our newfound power was how to eliminate recycling problems with the power of commitment and conscious choice. The Ten-Minute Heart Talk and the Ten-Minute Stuff Talk evolved out of this quest.

Ten minutes may not sound like much time to discuss important matters, whether they are matters of the Heart or the Stuff of life. That's where the structure of the process plays a significant role. The way the process is laid out allows people to go deeply very quickly. Couples who learn the process often report back to us their astonishment at how much deep connection can be generated in such a short time.

Speaking of astonishment, most couples are also amazed at how much intimacy the Stuff Talk creates. In fact, many couples have reported back to us that their Ten-Minute Stuff Talk was the key factor in helping them rebirth passion and ease in their relationship. There's a good reason for this: most people in relationships do not realize how much of their intimacy is being eaten up by scattering talk about Stuff throughout their conversations, day and night.

The Ten-Minute Stuff Talk

This simple conversation has extraordinary power. First, it gives you a way to organize a significant part of relationship life. In close relationships there will always be details about things that need to be done or fixed. The trick is to manage those details so they don't proliferate and block the flow of presence and intimacy in the relationship. Second, the Stuff Talk gives a big boost to your creativity. When we first started to do our own Stuff Talks in the early 1980s, we did it simply as an organizational tool. However, we quickly realized that the Stuff Talk also has great power as a facilitator of creativity. Without hiccups in the flow of intimacy caused by communication glitches around trivia, we found a deeper degree of connection with our creativity.

Necessary Trivia

The Ten-Minute Stuff Talk gives you a simple way to handle a category of life we call Necessary Trivia. For example, picking the right doorknobs for your dwelling is trivial but necessary. If you're passionate about interior decorating, getting the right doorknobs might not even seem trivial. In any case, it will need to be discussed at some point.

However, you don't need to start discussing it, as a couple in one of our seminars did, in the midst of making love. On the final day of a seminar there are often both tears and hilarity in the air, and there were both when Sharon and Ben shared a recent wake-up moment. They had been entwined in the midst of making love when suddenly one of them whispered, "Did you remember to look at the doorknob samples today?"

Oops. The other person had not remembered to look at the samples that day, and soon the lovers were on hiatus from intimacy and into a doorknob skirmish. That's an extreme example, but think of it as a metaphor for a habit we humans have: interrupting the flow of intimacy with communications about things we don't actually need to be talking about right then.

By cutting down on talking about Stuff at times when you could be enjoying intimacy, you open up new ways to connect and to receive support. With the Ten-Minute Stuff Talk, your main goal is to pack as much of the Stuff as possible into the ten minutes of the meeting, so that conversations about the trivial necessities of life don't get scattered throughout the day.

Get started with an essential preparatory step:

Make and Maintain a List

One key to successful Ten-Minute Stuff Talks is to keep a list between meetings so you can jot down the things you need to talk about during the ten minutes of the session. For example, we tend to do our Stuff meetings on Tuesday or Thursday evenings. If something comes up during the rest of the week, we write it down on a pad we keep for the occasion. Here's our list from a recent Stuff Talk between us:

- Materials for Creativity Camp
- Donations
- Gophers
- Transport to LA

We were deep into preparing for one of our favorite seminars of the year, our five-day immersion program in creativity. We put that up top because it branched off into a whole set of tasks that needed to be done. After we got that handled, we took a couple of minutes to decide whether to donate to some charitable organizations that had been soliciting us. Then we burrowed deeply into a conversation we'd had on other occasions: gophers. Until we moved to our now-beloved small town of Ojai in 2002, it's safe to say neither of us had given a minute's thought to the subject of gophers. We didn't give gophers any thought the first few years in Ojai either, because our backyard was so pristine that we often hosted neighborhood croquet games on its unblemished turf.

Then one day in glorious spring we walked out into our backyard and saw three massive mounds right in the middle of our manicured lawn.

We soon discovered a truism about our small town: if you want to get up a discussion with an Ojai resident, simply mention gophers or ants. Soon they will be sharing their frustrations and magical cures; if they really take a shine to you, they may even share the name of their Gopher Man, from the small brigade of specialists you go to when all else fails.

We'll save our ant struggles—now mercifully at truce for several years—for another occasion, but in the case of gophers we were back on the subject at the time we made that list. After many attempts to deal with the gophers through natural means such as herb plantings, benign gopher spray, and yes, even visualizations, we had come to the point at which we needed to select a Gopher Man. The one we liked best had said, "Yep, you got gophers all right. If it makes you feel any better, they probably came over from your neighbor's yard over there." It didn't make us feel any better to know where our gophers came from, but we appreciated his bluntness.

The last thing on the list was something that probably pops up at least once a month: choosing one of several different ways to get to Los Angeles. Whether it's Katie's car, Gay's car, train, or car service, the needs vary according to what we're going to be doing.

Making and keeping a list will help you avoid the trap of trying to remember it in your head, a trap that some say appears to widen as you mature into your later years. If you can possibly write it down, don't bother trying to remember it.

Here's the bottom line: if Stuff pops into your mind when you're having an easeful flow of intimacy with a mate or a friend—if you suddenly get an urge to discuss doorknobs in a moment of passion—ask yourself if it's urgent, like an overflowing bathtub or something else that needs to be handled on the spot. If it doesn't need to be dealt with at that moment to avoid catastrophe, jot it down to be covered in your next meeting.

Step-by-Step Instructions for a Ten-Minute Stuff Talk

Step One: Touch and Presence

Begin with a few moments of touch and presence so that you can remember the higher purpose of handling the details of chores and other trivial necessities: feeling a deeper and more harmonious flow of love and intimacy in your life.

Choose one of these options:

- Sit close enough so you can each have one hand on your heart and one hand on your partner's heart. Make sure you find a place to touch where you can rest your arm comfortably for a few moments.

- Sit side by side with each of you placing a hand on the other's abdomen or thigh. Find a comfortable place to rest.

Breathe together for a minute or so without talking. Enjoy being together. Appreciate each other's presence. Don't skip this step in your haste to get to the Stuff. Presencing is what it's all about and what clearing the Stuff will enhance, so favor presence first.

Step Two: The List

If you made a list beforehand of things to cover, bring the list out and add any other things to it you wish to discuss.

If you haven't made one beforehand, create a list now. When you have your list ready to go, pick the most important item first. If there's disagreement about what's most important, flip a coin. Then tick your way down the list, having what we call Conversations for Action.

Step Three: Conversations for Action

A Conversation for Action is a simple structure for getting things done on time. Essentially, you complete one sentence: **Who** agrees to do **what** by **when.**

Example:

Katie (who) agrees to get the handouts to the printer (what) by 5 P.M. Tuesday (when).

Gay (who) agrees to call John, our videographer (what), to arrange a planning meeting before noon tomorrow (when).

The Conversation for Action structure simplifies a major obstacle for partners: assuming that an agreement has occurred when actually nothing has been decided. If thinking or saying the following sentences sounds familiar, the Conversation for Action will radically change your life.

- "I thought you were picking up the dry cleaning."

- "You said you'd order those supplies before going to the gym."

- "Why is there no peanut butter in the refrigerator *again?!*"

- "Why do I always end up cleaning up?"

The Ten-Minute Stuff Talk is a way to simplify and declutter your life. You don't even need a partner to get value out of a Stuff Talk. Write out a list rather than carrying around your to-do list in your head. Dedicate a couple of times each week to sit yourself down and focus intently on your own Stuff. In other words, figure out what you need to get done and by when—it'll make your life a lot easier than letting your to-do's rattle around in your mind.

The Ten-Minute Heart Talk

The Ten-Minute Heart Talk is designed to give you a reliable, powerful way to deepen intimacy and move through issues that have an emotional charge to them. Whether you use it to explore decisions, solve problems, or savor positive feelings, the Heart Talk will bring you closer while honoring your individual perspectives and welcoming your uniqueness into the conversation.

Step-by-Step Instructions for a Ten-Minute Heart Talk

Step One: Touch and Presence

Choose one of these options:

- Sit across from each other, close enough so you can rest one hand on your heart and one hand on your partner's heart.

- Sit side by side with each of you placing a hand on the other's heart. If you can't comfortably put a hand on the other's chest, rest your hand on his or her thigh or simply sit close enough to be in physical contact with each other.

In either position, put a priority on comfort. Place your hands where they can comfortably rest for a little while. If your hands get tired, it's okay to take them away to rest for a few moments. As soon as fatigue has passed, return to touching your partner.

As you sit touching, focus on your own breathing for a minute or so, as your partner focuses on his or hers. Putting your awareness on your breathing helps you get centered and more open to connecting with your partner.

Enjoy a minute of breathing together without talking. After your minute of purely breathing together, move on to . . .

Step Two: Expressing Willingness and Commitment

Take a moment to each express your willingness and commitment to communicate everything that really needs to be communicated within the next ten minutes. It's important to get a "Yes" to that commitment, so that you don't unconsciously let a conflict go beyond your agreed-upon time limit.

Step Three: Feelings, Wants, and Needs

This step is the heart of the Heart Talk, your opportunity to communicate about the joys, angers, hurts, and fears that go on in the foreground and background of relationships. Do your best to communicate them from a position of healthy responsibility instead of blame. We suggest alternating speaking and listening, either sentence by sentence or using a timer to give each person equal communication time. Listener, this is an opportunity to deepen your presencing skills. You can practice turning toward your partner with an open posture, generating wonder rather than blame, breathing easily and moving so your body doesn't get stuck in familiar ruts. Listener, use the Heart Talk time to practice your Loop of Awareness to deepen your experience of presencing your inner world, your partner's expression, and the space between you. You can enhance your connection each time you engage in a Heart Talk.

Speaker, focus on two areas: feelings and wants/needs. To express feelings, say things like:

I'm so happy that . . .
I'm scared about . . .
I'm angry about . . .
I felt hurt when . . .

Avoid saying things like:

You never . . .
You always . . .
How could you . . .

In airing out all your feelings, make sure you devote plenty of those ten minutes to sharing positive feelings, things you appreciate about your partner, and good times you've had.

Communicate any wants and needs in the same straightforward way. Say things like:

Here's something I'd really like . . .
I'd like you to do _____ *instead of* _____.

Avoid saying things like:

You're never going to change, are you?
You're driving me nuts.
I want something for me for a change, since you always get everything you want!

The Heart Talk is designed to open and connect you both at an essence level. Sharing feelings and wants deepens your intimacy and sense of support. Having someone listen regularly to your evolving heart creates a kind of sweet closeness that can permeate your days and nights.

Step Four: Complete with Appreciation

It's important to make and keep meaningful agreements in any relationship. One way you can practice keeping your agreements is to be impeccable about maintaining your ten-minute time limit. However, sometimes you'll be in the middle of something important when your ten minutes are up. When that happens, handle it consciously by making a new agreement to continue the discussion. If you do that, though, both people have to want to continue. If you can't agree on whether or not to continue, schedule another Ten-Minute Heart Talk, perhaps later that day or the next day.

When you're finished with your ten minutes (or have scheduled a follow-up conversation), pause for another moment of silent connection. Tune in to your breathing. At the same time, be aware of your partner's breathing. Tune in to something you genuinely appreciate about your partner and express that out loud. Make it simple: "I appreciate . . ." Then express from your heart. Rest in connection for as long as you like before resuming your regular activities.

We highly recommend a regular experience of the Love Catalyst, detailed in Appendix A, to fill your intimacy reservoir and give your Heart Talks deeper resonance and power. You'll find that the Heart Talk and the Love Catalyst both support daily magic and spark the creative genius of your relationship. Remember, your experience of love, presence, and creativity can continue to grow throughout life. As many of our clients have confirmed, it just keeps getting better.

CHAPTER NINE

How to Attract a Conscious Loving Relationship

Caitlyn came to us at the age of 56. It was a year since the breakup of her second marriage, which had lasted six years. She was still heavyhearted about it.

"Is this the end of the line?" she asked us bluntly. "Should I forget about the whole relationship thing and just settle for what I have?"

"Which is?"

"I have a really good life, just with no man in it."

Caitlyn's situation was like that of many single people with whom we've worked. She had a good life going on her own, but she was feeling the ache of something missing from it. She was up against a barrier so significant we call it Barrier Number One.

Getting past Barrier Number One: Do You or Don't You?

The first barrier is when you haven't landed on actually *wanting* a lasting love relationship in your life right now. Part of you does, part of you doesn't. Perhaps without your even realizing it, this internal barrier is keeping you from success in the external quest to create lasting love in your life.

There is a solution to Barrier Number One—a way of clearing it out of the way. Best of all, it won't cost you a cent to get a lifetime supply of it. The solution is a special kind of *commitment*, a vow you make in the sacred depths of yourself. The power of this commitment releases you from the grip of despair and sends you into the future equipped with a foolproof navigation tool for your journey.

Picture yourself looking into the mirror and speaking a vow to your deepest self, a commitment that goes something like this:

I commit to attracting a loving relationship into my life, a love that lasts and grows over time.

Making that statement takes you off the bench and onto the field. That's where the action takes place. One big problem we've found is that single people send out mixed messages about whether or not they really want to manifest an intimate relationship. The even bigger problem is that most of them don't realize they're doing it. When you send out mixed messages, the most unconscious one is always the one people hear. For example, if ten minutes into a lunch date you decide you don't really like the person across from you, you're stuck with an unpleasant alternative. You could go radically blunt and say, "I've decided I don't really like you. Let's finish eating by ourselves." Most people, though, opt for a more conventional approach: you go ahead and finish lunch in a polite manner, while pretending your attitude of "I don't really want to be here" isn't there lurking in the background. The trouble with this approach is that attempting to silence or ignore your genuine feelings often makes the other person perceive them even more loudly and clearly.

A sincere commitment breaks that spell. When you make a sincere vow to your deepest self and the universe around you, something like "I commit to creating the relationship of my dreams in real life," you come off the bench and onto the field.

Getting Through Barrier Number Two: Settling for Less

Don't stop there, though. There's another key commitment you can make to amp up your manifestation power.

Picture yourself again looking into the mirror and making a second sincere vow:

*I specifically commit never to
settle for less than what I really want.*

This commitment is just as important as the first one; settling for less than what you really want in relationships is a virulent plague in the 21st century. To avoid the plague, you'll not only need to make a sincere vow never to settle for less, you'll also need to do some clear thinking about what you want and don't want.

We spent the better part of a morning working with Caitlyn on these issues. As we heard more of her relationship history, it spelled out a pattern of undervaluing herself, leading to settling for less. She repeatedly put herself in relationships with men that caused her to lose both self-respect and money. What she had put up with—from bankruptcy to drunk-tank bailouts to catching a new husband in bed with the maid of honor—astonished even us.

She also had to face an issue from her past that was causing her to be ambivalent about creating a new relationship. During the whole year since the breakup, she had never simply sat with her grief and felt it consciously. Instead she'd kept herself busy by joining three different singles websites, corresponding with and rejecting "more than a hundred men" on the various sites, and even putting a highly detailed personal ad in the newspaper.

To change the pattern, we first asked Caitlyn to devote a few moments to being with the grief through Full-Spectrum Presencing. "Take a few easy breaths and feel the places in your body where you still feel sad about the breakup." Once she slowed down to honor her authentic feelings for a moment, her mood visibly brightened. She said, "Oh, wait, I think I just made a connection."

At a certain point in each relationship she would start to bottle up feelings out of fear of causing conflict. Invariably, after a while the bottle would pop, leading to noisy conflicts of the sort she feared most. As she explored the issue she realized it was the central drama in her parents' ongoing battle, which led to their divorce when she was five years old. Both her parents would hide their feelings until a blowout occurred every week or two. By the time they divorced, Caitlyn had soaked up so much of the pattern by osmosis that she repeated it unwittingly in her adult relationships.

Getting over Barrier Number Three: Placing Your Order

Full-Spectrum Presencing opened the gate for Caitlyn, but she also needed to do some "real world" work on attracting a new relationship into her life. In our work with singles, we have found that in order to attract a quality relationship, they need to identify at least three things they want and three things they don't want.

Most people repeat old destructive patterns because they haven't made a clear commitment to something better. At midlife and beyond, the pressure intensifies to break free of these patterns. One common pattern is to know what you don't want but not know what you want. Another common pattern is the opposite: you're clear about what you want but haven't given conscious thought to what you don't want.

So if you're single, check in with yourself. Are you clear on the top three things you want in a close relationship and the top three things you don't want? If so, take a moment to review them right now. If not, get clear right now by asking:

What is the #1 thing that's important for me to have in a lasting love relationship? Perhaps it's honesty or freedom or a sense of shared beliefs—everyone's #1 is slightly different from others'. What's yours?

Do the same for your #2 and #3 most important things to have in a close relationship.

If you've already gotten clear about the three things you most *don't* want to repeat in your next relationship, review them now. If not, start by asking:

What is the absolute most important thing I never want to have in a relationship again? Perhaps it's that you never want to be in a relationship with an addict again, or that you never want to be with someone who doesn't like kids again. Whatever your three biggest "don't want's" are, make a list of them so you're absolutely clear about them.

It's like when you set off on a trip. If you're absolutely clear you want to visit Chicago, Calcutta, and Copenhagen, and you also know for absolute sure you *don't* want to go to Borneo, Brisbane, and the Bronx, your chances of ending up where you want to be are greatly enhanced.

Sometimes you need to be forceful in stating a "don't want." Certain relationship problems are toxic and need to be avoided, like an allergen. For example, Gay is allergic to sesame seeds and sesame oil, which he learned the hard way from his first trip to a Chinese restaurant when he was a kid. "Now, when I order in a restaurant, I go out of my way to ask if there is sesame involved. I also don't handle MSG or peanut oil well, so I usually ask that they not be used either. I eventually even found a Chinese restaurant that caters to finicky people. The first time I went there, I asked my inevitable question to the waiter. He drew himself up in pride and said, 'Sir, there has never been MSG or sesame oil on our premises.'" We think you should be just that finicky about your love life.

Ordering up a lasting love relationship is like ordering a meal, but with one specific difference; you need to be clear about what you want and don't want. When you order in a restaurant, you don't usually need to list what you don't want, unless you have experienced toxicity in some past relationship with an item. You can just say, "Short stack of blueberry pancakes, two eggs on the side, over medium," as Gay did on a recent visit to Bonnie Lu's Country Café, and with three simple, positive commands you can get the breakfast you want.

Relationships are different, because for relationships to succeed, you need to be really clear about what you don't want. More strongly put, you need to be clear about what you absolutely will not put up with. You might have a list of more than three things fitting that description, but we've found it useful to start with a sturdy foundation of three.

Caitlyn's three positive "wants" were 1) we have respect and admiration for each other, 2) we're best friends as well as married to each other, and 3) we have fun together. In past relationships she'd had glimpses of those qualities but had never put them all together in one relationship.

Caitlyn's three "don't wants" were simple, straightforward, and obviously based on a lot of painful life experience. She didn't want anybody in her life with 1) financial problems, 2) addiction issues, or 3) a history of cheating.

The Ultimate Step

The ultimate step in freeing yourself from the past is also the ultimate step in opening yourself to a new mate in your life. It only takes a split second to take the step, but it has such power that it influences every one you take from then on. It's the moment when you love yourself unconditionally, exactly as you are, for everything you've done and not done. It's the moment when you love yourself for being alone, the forgiving gift to yourself of celebrating your singularity.

In other words, a crucial step in attracting a new relationship into your life is to love yourself thoroughly for being single right now.

Tune in as Caitlyn takes that step:

Katie: Everything we've talked about points to one thing you feel is unlovable about yourself. What is that? When you tune in deep down inside, what is that one thing that you find hardest to love in yourself?

Caitlyn: I guess it's a feeling that I'm never enough.

Gay: Tell us some more about that.

Caitlyn: No matter what I do, and whatever I achieve, there's some part of me that feels like I don't deserve it, like if they knew who I really was they'd take it all back.

Katie: Ah, yes. I've felt that one myself more than once.

Caitlyn: You have?

Gay: I have too. It comes with the territory.

Caitlyn: What territory?

Gay: The territory of being human. Just about everybody is going to feel that from time to time, especially if they're high achievers like you are. One of the hidden motivations that drive a lot of successful people is a fear they're fundamentally bad or undeserving and need to prove they're not.

Katie: So go ahead right now and love the place in yourself that feels most unlovable.

Caitlyn: So, you want me to love something I can't love? That's weird.

Katie: Yes, it's definitely weird. But do it anyway. Close your eyes and follow my suggestions inside. First, softly say out loud the day it is. "Today is Tuesday." Then pause and notice your whole-body experience for a few seconds. Say "Today is Tuesday" again and pause, noticing the whole-body feeling of acceptance that today is Tuesday. You might not care or have an opinion about the day, but you can tune in to the experience of accepting. Now give that same acceptance to your not-good-enough-ness. (Caitlyn's breath deepens and expands as she begins to move into acceptance.)

Katie: Now, Caitlyn, imagine sitting with your not-good-enough-ness on a porch swing, the kind of porch swing that moves in the most delicious, welcoming rhythm. You're sitting with the not-good-enough part of you just as you would with a close friend who's going through something painful. You're being with, sensing, including.

Give your not-good-enough part the same presence you would a good friend. (The corners of Caitlyn's mouth start to turn up into a smile, and her forehead creases relax.)

Katie: Now let yourself think of a person or place that you know you love, that you love without any conditions. Let that person or place easily emerge in your awareness and open to feeling the body experience of loving. When you can tune in to your experience of loving, give it to your not-enough place. Let it wash over or shine on or embrace your not-good-enough-ness just as it is right now. You can do that whenever not-good-enough comes up and for as long as you like. (A couple of tears well up in Caitlyn's eyes as they open.)

Caitlyn: I've never let myself get close enough to that place inside to actually love it. I feel as though I've just gotten pounds lighter.

It doesn't matter if you love the unlovable in yourself for ten seconds or a tenth of a second—once you've felt it, even for a moment, you've opened the secret door to creating relationship magic.

Take a moment right now to feel the power of this new state of consciousness we're referring to. First, let go of expectation: if you're single, release the idea that you ought to have a mate. Let go of any other future-facing fantasies you might have about your love life.

Then, let go of whatever has gone on in the past. Everything that happened is beyond your control now. Nothing you can do can change it. The healing move that allows you to go beyond the pain of the past is to accept it fully, as it is. Release your urge to want it to be different. Let it be. You can use Unhooking the Source from Appendix A whenever you like, to hone your letting-go skills.

When you free yourself from the future and the past, you are free to innovate *now*. Your energy is no longer tied up in wanting the past to be different or the future to be any preconceived way. You're in the present, this very moment, an open opportunity to create your new life.

Now all you have to do is add a light intention to this open state of consciousness. A light intention is a gentle aiming of your energy in a certain direction. We call it a "light intention" to distinguish it from a heavy intention such as "I've got to manifest a mate or else my life means nothing." All you need to do is nudge the universe in the direction of sending you the right sort of mate for you. At the same time, let yourself and the universe know that you are going to be just fine without one, that the growing love and respect you have for yourself is big enough to embrace yourself whether you are solo or mated.

There is powerful magic in setting intentions like that. We've been privy to many such moments when people have sent their lives off in a new direction, affording us a rich supply of examples of what happened in the aftermath.

A New Paradigm

The new paradigm we want singles to embrace is a process of easeful attraction rather than stressful pursuit. In our seminars and our office, we've heard hundreds of single people tell tales of the lengths they've gone to in pursuit of a satisfying love life. Some of those tales were amusing, others harrowing (such as one seminar participant who saw a picture in the paper of the serial killer Ted Bundy and realized to her horror that she had dated him briefly several years earlier).

Here are some examples from our students and clients of stressful dating strategies gone awry:

Early on in my relationship with Tom, I wanted to make everything perfect. I set up a twilight picnic with all the trimmings, including candles, wine, appetizers . . . highly romantic. . . *then*, as I was working hard on the romantic part, I completely left my connection with myself and dumped the wine glasses, then the wine bottle, then set my sweatshirt on fire when I leaned into a candle, *then* stabbed him in the hand with the knife I was using to cut up pears as he reached over for some cheese or chocolate or something . . . then criticized myself to kingdom come! Seems that I was still rather daft, as I continued in relationship with him despite all the signals to *get out* . . . for another three years. This would have made a great comedy skit! (It was only funny to me a good while later.)

What I've noticed in a few of my single friends is a choice to "date" several people—which can mean anything from having dinner together many times to hooking up regularly—while working on manifesting their ideal mate. The logic behind this has something to do with "not getting desperate or having the scent of desperation." What I see happening instead or also is a kind of lukewarm radar going out around availability, and a lot of energy used up in compromise. This appears to be the opposite of the long list. This is the no-list, the "I'm super chill and have lots of lovers" approach. Which can be way more complicated and stressful than it sounds.

Well, I can connect with men as people who are fun and interesting and that's easy and great! When I start thinking about long-term commitment, or him being "the one," it's like the alien within overtakes me and I start playing push and pull games. "Is he good enough? Am I good enough?" goes through my head! Do the logistics work? Do our passions support one another? Does he inspire me? My mom says, "You're looking for too much in a man—they just help you lift heavy things once in a while." Till I say, "Okay, let's just be friends with benefits"—wooh, then I'm safe!

Many years ago I did a vision board that was way too detailed. I put a photo of a big baby right in the center, thinking I wanted a child. Well, what I got was a big ol' cry baby of a man. Learned my lesson on that one . . .

I am laughing, as my "strategy" for dating has often looked like a strategy *not* to date, instead to focus so intently on other things that I don't let myself want to date or even hardly think about it. I have, on several occasions, created hiking first dates, where I honestly took myself *power* hiking to see if the guy could keep up with me . . . guess what happened? I've also been on a variety of first dates where in addition to looking for what I could appreciate, I was looking for how he totally *wasn't* right for me. I looked for flaws, kinks in the system, reasons to say no. I also have my persona who walks around asking, "Are you my lover?" like that children's book *Are You My Mother?* I've made up stories about why different men are/are not my lover and then not done anything about the ones I am attracted to.

I had gone through the arduous process of an online dating site—thousands of questions, then the question exchange, the values, the pictures, etc. When I received an e-mail from him, I had an internal "No, I don't think so" but couldn't find a reason why not (he seemed attractive, my age, employed). I agreed to go out. On our first date, I showed up at the restaurant. He had arrived earlier and was sitting at the bar. As I approached him and introduced myself I couldn't help but notice his shoes—sneakers: but not just any sneakers, sneakers with Velcro instead of laces. I judged myself with the thought *You don't know, he could have some wrist issue or fine motor skills.* As the date progressed through appetizers, I learned he lived with his 80-year-old mother (again my thought was *Well, maybe he is caring for her as she is dying or something*). By the time the entrees arrived, I learned his friend circle was mostly her friends and bingo and church. Before dessert I was saying good-bye because I couldn't censor any longer and asked about the shoes. Sure enough, they were easier to get on and off—hmmmm.

Attacking genuine love [we left this typo in on purpose, as it caused great hilarity when the writer realized what she'd unconsciously written] is wonderful, and doing the three yeses and nos is vital. One also needs to remember to be explicitly clear with the universe. Another friend went through the attracting genuine love process and tuning in to her yeses and nos. After four months she realized she had manifested all the qualities except they were within her new dog. She didn't clarify human versus canine.

At the other end of the spectrum from stressful pursuit is the flat state of passivity that comes from having given up. We've talked to many single people who have alternated back and forth between pursuit and passivity for years. The new paradigm cures that problem, because in it you shift to a more expansive state of consciousness, one that transcends the suffering caused by going back and forth between pursuit and passivity. This expanded state takes you beyond the grasp of expectation and the slack of despair. Into the space of openness and positive intention, you can now attract genuine love.

CHAPTER TEN

Conscious Loving
Online

When we're interviewed on television or elsewhere, we're often asked some version of this question: "Are relationships easier or harder now that people can communicate by text and videophones and all the new technology?" Our answer is: Yes. In other words, it's both easier and harder. Gay's grandparents told him that when they were separated during the Spanish-American War, their letters sometimes took months to go back and forth between them. Now you can push a button in California and send an *I love you* and the sound of a kiss to your beloved's phone in Calcutta. The new technology makes it easier to connect with other people, but that's also what makes it harder. Because there are so many ways to communicate, it makes it even more important to communicate simply and from the heart.

Never before in human history has the air around us been so full of trivial messages, the OMGs, LOLs, and WTFs that buzz back and forth among the six billion cell phones now on earth. At the same time, the new technology gives us an expanding universe of ways to say the things that really need to be said.

Logging On

On a trip to Jordan a few years ago, we passed a lone sheep-herder tending his flock on a hillside. Pausing to savor this ancient pastoral scene, we took a closer look and noticed that the shepherd was texting on his smartphone. For all we know, the shepherd might have been communicating with a potential mate he met online at lonesomesheepherders.com.

One aspect of the new world we live in is the remarkable proliferation of online dating sites for mature single, divorced, and widowed people. The growth in online dating and computer-aided relationship enhancement has changed the dynamics of both singles' and couples' relationships in the 21st century. For example, the two largest online dating sites (Match.com and eHarmony. com) have nearly 40 million members, approximately 10 million of whom are in the mature demographic of 45 and up. In addition, a number of new sites, such as OurTime.com, focus exclusively on the midlife and over demographic.

Here's a clue to how big the phenomenon is: the number of people aged 45 to 75 who start dating each other online now exceeds those who meet and start dating at work or school. That number is especially remarkable considering that online dating didn't exist a generation ago. Studies also show that approximately two out of every three people over 50 will eventually try online dating.

So, even though you may not be deeply immersed in the digital world—putting hours into your social media and tweeting pictures of your lunch to your followers—it is increasingly likely that you will meet and interact with potential mates in the online realm. About a third of marriages now begin with an online connection; this number is sure to grow. If you're online now, this chapter can help you refine your presence so as to maximize your chances of attracting a conscious, loving mate. If you're not yet online, we aim to inspire you to get there, showing you a few simple guidelines to assist you in navigating the new world successfully. By the way, you may find these suggestions useful offline as well.

Getting Through Fear

Many of us have fears about online dating. You may fear that you don't really know the person you're communicating with or that they could be completely misrepresenting themselves. Consider, though, that these possibilities all exist in our everyday lives as well. Were you to begin dating someone in a more traditional way, you would still be taking an inherent risk. If you truly desire to meet someone, stepping out into the world is a necessary step, whether you choose to take that risk online or in the physical world.

Take a moment now to scan through the different fears you might have about online dating. Your goal is to embrace your fear, not to get rid of it. Take time to explore any fears you might have, with an attitude of loving curiosity.

Is your fear based on some real-life occurrence in the past? If so, ask yourself if there is anything you can do right now to put that past experience to rest. If you can't think of any right-now actions to take, consciously release it, like you might shrug off a heavy backpack of burden you've been carrying on your shoulders.

Starting Out

If you are ready to try your hand (and your heart) at online dating, you'll find in this chapter some of the methods we recommend you employ. Throughout the chapter, keep in mind that as with dating in a traditional sense, safety is important when it comes to online dating as well. Don't divulge personal financial information or anything else that you wouldn't want exposed over the Internet. Also, if you do plan on meeting someone in person whom you've connected with online, be sure to do so in a public place, at least the first time you meet.

As you'll quickly realize in online dating, there are a number of different dating sites to choose from and myriad different personality types on the different sites. Each site offers different benefits and a different interface. Before you create a profile, take time to explore the features of a few sites before choosing the one that is best for you. You may want to create a profile on a couple of sites at once. Over time, you'll likely develop a preference for one over the other. Make sure to keep your profile information consistent across any and all profiles you have. There are many users who maintain multiple profiles; the last thing you want is for someone to discover inconsistencies in the way you present yourself just as you are getting to know them.

People often ask us to recommend specific dating sites, but we hesitate to do so because new ones are always emerging. Our clients have used all the big sites such as Match, eHarmony, and OurTime. New sites come online frequently, so be on the lookout for emerging possibilities.

With cautions expressed, let's find out what it takes to maximize your online dating experience. Based on conversations we've had with clients who had strongly positive experiences that led to lasting relationships, there are a handful of key intentions that increase the likelihood of online success.

Intention One: Be Creative

Hardly anything feels more awkward than a boring first date. Think back on any unpleasant dating experience (and most of us have surely had at least a few of them). What were the things you didn't like? Did your date talk only about his or her own interests? Did your date focus on the negative? These are mistakes you don't want to repeat in your own online dating profile. After all, this is your only chance at making a first impression, and you want to make it count.

Writing about your interests is important, as people are often drawn to those with similar interests as themselves, but do so anecdotally, without overwhelming your potential mate. Remember, we as humans have a finite attention span. You'll want to capture interest quickly. Mention things that interest you, but also let people know that they can ask you questions if they'd like to get to know you a little better.

Being creative will require some effort on your part. If you're lucky, your perfect match will search you out and reach out to you. However, you should be open to searching for others who may interest you as well. Be open to meeting new types of people, and if you come across a profile that sparks your interest, reach out to that person.

Write a personal message that shows you have read their personal profile. Nobody likes getting a recycled message that was sent to dozens of other users as well. For example, if you come across a profile of someone who interests you and they mention rock climbing as one of their interests, you may want to mention something about that in your message to that person. Whether you have gone rock climbing in the past, have plans to in the future, or have no interest in the hobby, it shows that you at least took time to learn more about the individual you are writing to before writing the message.

If you receive a response to one of your messages, be sure to take time to read the response and give thoughtful answers to any questions they may have asked. Continue to ask questions and try to learn more about one another the same way you would were you to be going on a date in person. If you feel that things are progressing well, you may want to consider asking your new flame out on an online "date." This works great if you are separated by a long distance or if you don't feel ready to meet in person quite yet. Some good ideas include watching a movie together online, talking over Skype or another video chat service, and playing a game online. Seeing how someone behaves during competition will provide good insight into the person's character.

It's important to show your creative side in any new relationship. Remember, creativity comes in many forms. For some of us, it is about appreciating art, while for others it comes in the form of creating it. We all have a creative side, whether we recognize it or not. Meeting someone who draws that creativity out of us is a genuine treasure.

Here's a great example of a creative profile, which we received from its author, Karen Thompson. Not only is it deep, revealing, and fun to read, it also had the desired effect: she got the kind of man she was looking for!

I'm back online after a hiatus of several years. I see this as an opportunity to hang my shingle again and shout out to the world that I am available!

My friends describe me as loyal, generous, playful, driven, quirky, younger than my chronological age. I see myself as fun-loving and mature, optimistic and grounded, sensual and earthy, as well as smart and creative. I'm most comfortable in the company of very smart, creative, and driven men and I am looking forward to co-creating a masterpiece of a partnership in this divine life with my amazing man when he finally shows up. Could he be you??

I have been spending most of my time in recent years in the earnest pursuit of building my business and successfully raising my now 18-year-old daughter. Now that she is well on her way, I find that I have some pretty significant energy to devote to myself, my work, and my future partnership. I am better than ever and find that I have the time and space to enjoy *my* life again. I'd love the company of an amazing man on my journey.

I often describe myself as a sociable introvert. I love people and have devoted my life to making the world a better place, for sure. Yet I also crave downtime alone to replenish and refresh myself on a regular basis. And so, my perfect partnership respects and honors our individuality as well as our togetherness. I'm imagining that you are a professional man, perhaps working in one of the creative domains, and are, like me, at the top of your game in your industry and love what you do. You have room for our relationship in your life and might even be interested in collaborating on a project or two with me along the way. Family is important to you, as it is with me. We both have developed healthy boundaries and have learned how to say no as well as yes in life. I am really looking to meet the man who is to be my life partner. When we meet we are both exceedingly grateful for our mutual big love, which proves to be of deep service somehow, some way, in our hearts and also in the world. Our relationship is good for our kids too. We create a loving partnership and home that nourishes our souls as well as our family.

I realize that my vision is not for everyone! Many of you may be interested in dating around and experiencing lots of different people. No worries about that. You see, I only want one man. So, if my profile resonates and seems to be in the realm of what you too are envisioning for your life, give me a shout and we can see where it goes. And, for all who read my profile, may Grace shine upon you as you navigate the sometimes treacherous waters of the dating world. Blessings to you on your path.

That profile brought tears to our eyes when we first read it. We appreciated how transparent Karen was about her life and what she wanted. The way she closed her communication also touched us. It seemed especially thoughtful to extend a blessing to her readers, wishing them well on their journey. We liked the way it focused on giving as well as receiving.

Intention Two: Be Authentic

Karen's profile is also an example of a second intention we think is important in online dating. No matter what you do, stay in integrity by representing yourself accurately to the world. Your authentic self is the greatest gift you have, and it's important that you use that gift in attracting a mate who's right for you.

Authenticity is about both speaking and listening. Relationships work best when you are presenting your authentic self to the other person and listening to his or her authentic self. Listening to what the other person has to say and showing genuine interest will play as important a role in how the relationship moves forward as what you say about yourself. In other words, genuine give and take is where the action is, asking questions of each other and listening thoughtfully to each other's responses. If you feel that interest begins to fade after a while or that your enthusiasm for your date's interests is not being reciprocated, be open and honest about your feelings without blaming the other person for it or becoming angry.

By bringing it up, you may realize that it is not a perfect match and you can both move on, bringing you one step closer to finding your Prince or Princess Charming. However, you may find that when you're open and honest about the way you feel, your date will respond with renewed interest. People often respond favorably to genuine displays of authentic feeling.

It is important as well to keep your own likes and dislikes in mind when getting to know someone online. You may have criteria that are very important to you. For example, if you have children it is often very important to you that anyone you date likes children. If you learn that someone you are talking to does not like to be around children, it may be easier to move on from the dating opportunity in the early stages after learning this than it would be later on in the relationship.

Some of the most painful and long-lasting relationship dramas come from overriding initial reservations, missing early signals that the relationship isn't destined for harmony. An extreme example from our files gives you the picture:

> A woman—an experienced therapist in her late 40s—watches with astonishment and disapproval as a man pauses during their initial date to brighten up his personality with a snort of cocaine. However, in spite of her revulsion at this public display of practically everything she doesn't want in a relationship, a little voice in her head whispers, "My love can save him from his excesses." Fourteen years later, she finally gives up trying to reform him and gets a divorce.

We have dozens of such examples, and they all go pretty much the same way: Something—and often something major—is politely overlooked or swept under the tablecloth at the beginning of the relationship. Inevitably, though, it doesn't stay swept for very long. It reappears, often when least expected. Painful drama then ensues.

You can prevent a lot of painful drama by getting clear up front about what your relationship priorities are, especially as you fill out forms and make choices about your profile and other categories. In Appendix A, The Love Catalyst for Singles, we'll show you how to create three absolute yeses and three absolute nos. This is the simplest and most effective tool we've found for clarifying your intentions. If you know, down in the deepest reaches of your being, what you want and don't want, you send out clear signals to other people.

While you may have some big, deal-breaker differences, it's important to leave plenty of room in your relationship life for individual differences. Individual differences are one of the elements of a relationship that give it flavor. Learning to handle those differences gives much-needed practice in expanding our hearts to embrace the unfamiliar.

We have a name for the emergence of individual differences in a relationship: the Sushi Factor. We named it in honor of our many clients who have had repeated conflicts over the subject of raw fish. We keep a running list of the relationship problems people bring to our seminars and office. The top five categories (in this order) are:

- Money
- Chores
- Sex
- Children
- Food

By far the greatest number of food conflicts we ever hear about concern sushi. Conflicts between vegetarians and meat eaters run second, with spicy food conflagrations in third place. The typical sushi argument goes like this: Person A in the relationship is absolutely wild about sushi, can't get enough of it; Person B absolutely can't stand it, may even find the sight of it revolting. Drama ensues, sometimes perpetuated through decades.

Under normal circumstances, you might think the solution is simple and straightforward: the partner who loves sushi (or bowling or fishing or anything else the other person can't stand) simply goes about their business, enjoying their raw fish, bowling, and fishing. Meanwhile, the sushi-phobe simply enjoys something else. However, as everyone from Shakespeare to country-song crooners have lamented, love and relationships are not normal circumstances. In one extreme case, the argument about sushi went on so long that the partner who loved sushi eventually lost his taste for it! By contrast, another couple devised a brilliant solution that usually involved going to two different restaurants in the same night, the order to be determined by coin toss.

The best attitude to take toward the Sushi Factor is to welcome the emergence of differences. Individual differences—not big enough to be deal breakers—often come at you rapidly in a new relationship. If you are aware that this occurs, you're in a much better position to devise creative solutions.

Intention Three: Guard Your Integrity Zealously

Integrity is something to keep front and center in your consciousness throughout your online dating experience. Be honest about who you are, your faults and weaknesses as well as your accomplishments and strengths. The ability to be proud of who you are while being honest about your mistakes is an attractive quality to many suitors looking for an ideal mate. It establishes trust from the get-go.

For example, avoid making one of the most common mistakes people make in their online profiles: posting overly flattering pictures of themselves. Authenticity is one of your foundation strengths; the last thing you want to do is set up unrealistic expectations. While you may have success attracting people to your profile by using a picture of yourself in a thong bikini from ten years ago, the shock value upon meeting the real person might quell your potential mate's desire. Any trust you had developed will be tarnished when the person realizes that you misrepresented yourself online.

Money is another area to be honest about. Don't claim to make millions of dollars if that is not the case. Don't claim great athletic prowess if you haven't worked out in ten years, either. These untruths will eventually be exposed, with potential heartache for both parties.

One of the most important reasons to be honest about who you are is that it shows a healthy sense of confidence. Confidence is a quality that is attractive to all sexes and creates a healthy platform to build a relationship on. It's not the same as arrogance, which is one of the big turnoffs in both online and offline dating. In preparing this book, we asked people to send us examples of singles profiles they enjoyed reading and the ones they didn't like. Arrogance, any display of hyped self-worth born of insecurity, was a common element in the profiles people didn't like.

Intention Four: Be Realistic and Unrealistic All at the Same Time

Whether you believe in love at first sight or not, it's not something that happens every day. The ratio holds true in online dating as well. Don't expect to find the man or woman of your dreams within the first hour of creating your profile. More than likely, you'll end up talking to a number of different people before you meet someone who really interests you. Take mental notes about the things you do and do not like when getting to know some of these people. You may realize that some of the things you don't like about the way certain people interact are things that you yourself may be doing.

Be realistic about your expectations online as well. Nobody is perfect, although some people may try to pretend they are, which is not a good online dating habit. You may find that you are getting along well with someone and learn after a while that there are certain things they do, or have done in the past, that are not to your liking. Remember that dating is a two-way street and there may be certain less-than-desirable characteristics you have as well. Hopefully you don't write people off in your personal life for one flaw. The same should be said for online dating. If it's something that is a deal breaker, one of your absolute nos, that is one thing. But if not, you may want to consider bringing it up to the person and sharing your authentic experience. They may not even realize they are doing it. Your choice to share rather than withhold may completely open up your connection or may help them not repeat the same behavior if it doesn't work out between the two of you. If you do decide to go your separate ways, take the opportunity to let the person know it was nice getting to know them. You may even want to ask them if there was anything you did that rubbed them the wrong way. It may be uncomfortable at first, but it could prove valuable in regard to making a good impression on the next person you meet online.

At the same time you're being realistic, keep in mind the insight of the author Roald Dahl: "Those who don't believe in magic will never find it." In other words, be open to creating totally unrealistic results. Sometimes magic actually does happen in online connections. The numbers don't lie—half of all relationships and a third of marriages now begin online. It's an opportunity that did not exist 30 years ago. Here's to taking advantage of it with clarity of intent.

Intention Five: Be Blame Free

You may have past relationships that ended with wounded feelings and worse. Most of us probably have. In your online connections and elsewhere, resist the urge to bad-mouth any of your exes. When we surveyed people about their online experiences, we found that one of the biggest turnoffs was hearing a date say negative things about former partners.

You'll naturally want to talk about past relationships at some point in getting to know a new potential partner. Inevitably you'll need to talk about how and why past relationships ended. If you claim responsibility for your part in why the relationship ended, you show a level of maturity that many people will be attracted to.

On the other hand, if you get caught up in aiming blame at someone from the past, you present yourself to new potential partners as a victim. Caution! The most troublesome kinds of relationships come when two people bond as fellow victims. Relationships of this type typically have continuous conflict of a particularly toxic kind: each person has to keep proving that he or she is a bigger victim than the other.

It's a big challenge to take responsibility for how a relationship ended, but it's especially difficult if it ended as a result of your partner's infidelity or another similar mistreatment. In some life circumstances, you get treated so badly that there's unanimous agreement in your family and friendship circle that you are the victim and the other person the perpetrator. How do you get out of what one of our clients called "the compassion trap" of having all your friends treat you as having no responsibility in the matter? In our experience, you can only get to these heroic levels of responsibility by asking big questions of yourself, questions that are gentle and tough at the same time:

Hmmm, even though the Supreme Court would probably unanimously agree that I was the victim in this situation, what can I learn from it that makes the whole experience useful to me?

Hmmm, do I have a theme going here? Have similar situations happened to me in the past?

One sign you've moved on emotionally from a past relationship is when you've transformed blame into learning. With that in mind, be sure to ask a very big question:

Hmmm, what did I learn from the experience that will allow me to give and receive more love in my life?

Be open and honest about your life's priorities from the beginning. Nothing can sour a relationship faster than setting up unrealistic expectations. If you are someone who is very dedicated to your work, make that known early on. You'll want to let the person you're talking to know that work is a priority for you so that later on in the relationship they don't feel rejected when you choose to continue dedicating a lot of time to it.

Be forthcoming about all the important relationships in your life. If you have a best friend of the opposite sex, let your potential partner know that early on in the process of getting to know them. It will give them insight into your life and make them feel less threatened by the relationship later on. If you have close relationships with siblings, children, or grandchildren, make sure to share these things as well. It will show that you are a well-rounded person and are able to maintain close relationships while also letting the person feel that you are comfortable sharing an intimate part of your life with them.

Intention Six: Be Present

Presencing is such an important practice that we gave it a chapter all on its own. It bears mentioning again in an online context. Presencing is about standing free of the past and future, open to all the positive possibilities of the current moment. It's about appreciating all that is being offered to you in a given situation.

One client posted sticky notes on her computer to remind her of the intentions she wanted to keep foremost in her mind in online dating. She said, "The one that made the biggest difference was the one that I'd written in big, bold letters: BE PRESENT." In that spirit, do your best to appreciate yourself and every individual you come across in your online dating experience. Take time to think about who the person is and what interests them, and respond thoughtfully when answering questions or striking up a conversation.

Take time getting to know someone. Keep in mind that it is not a race. You'll want to think carefully throughout the process about whether or not a particular relationship is beneficial for both parties. Be open and honest about your feelings without blaming anyone for the way you feel. If you sense that it is time to move on, do so with appreciation for having gotten to know someone new. Wish them well and dive back into your online dating excursion with a renewed sense of promise.

The Internet allows you to sort through thousands upon thousands of possible dates and mates. While it affords a profusion of opportunities that didn't exist a few decades before now, it can also be overwhelming. That's why it's helpful to keep these essential intentions in the forefront of your consciousness.

Regardless of which website you use, what Sushi Factors you decide to reject or embrace, and whether you connect with a lot of new people or just the one who matters most, may your quest for lasting love be enhanced magnificently by the digital tools available in the new world!

Afterword

Loving relationships can become heirlooms that we inherit in our own lifetimes, shining with the patina of many harmonious choices made and radiant with expanding creativity. If you come back to these tools and weave them into your daily life, we predict that you'll continue discovering the genius of your unique essence and the genius of your loving relationships.

Once you've decided to turn your days into a living laboratory of expansion, presence, integrity, and play, you stand free of time and breathe freely in the continuous re-creation that deep connection provides. Each day ripples with the curiosity you generate and the wonder you bring to all your relating. We celebrate your choices, your loving heart, and your willingness to continue becoming. Thank you for taking the journey with us and for turning your love into a work of art.

Appendix A

Six Whole-Body Learning Activities for Couples, Singles, and Professionals

In this section you'll find detailed experiential processes that complement the activities you've found throughout the book. These processes tend to take longer than the ones you've read about so far. Dive into them at a time when you have 20 minutes or more to devote to experiencing them. We think the investment is worth your time.

Why do we include an extensive series of processes in this book? Because whole-body learning works. Hundreds of partners have shared with us that just talking about an issue doesn't create lasting change or lasting love. A growing body of research supports what we discovered decades ago—body intelligence, or BQ, expands your love IQ.

Body intelligence is the direct, consciously felt experience of being alive, from the flow of blood and sensation to the many attitudes and mental shifts that weave with our responses to being in a body in relationships, work, and the world. The most common complaint that Katie received in her practice as a therapist was "I don't know what I'm feeling" or "I just don't feel." She took this to mean more than "I don't experience emotions." Rather, this common complaint is the predictable apotheosis of 2,000+ years of culture and religion casting the body as bad, wrong, immoral, and untrustworthy. We humans have been taught to fear our bodies and not listen to our bodies' messages, as though we'd turn into hedonistic gluttons if we did. The inventor of the light bulb, Thomas Edison, famously declared, "The chief function of the body is to carry the brain around."

Consider instead the perspective of Joseph Campbell: "I think that what we're seeking is an experience of being alive, so that our life experiences on the purely physical plane will have resonances within our own innermost being and reality, so that we actually feel *the rapture of being alive*." (Emphasis ours.) People must first come into their bodies to experience them, rather than proceeding through life as James Joyce described his character Mr. Duffy, who "lived at a little distance from his body." When we value what our body is communicating to us, we open the doors to a level of vitality that cannot be achieved by just thinking about things. Every *body* has a different road map, and by becoming intimate with what our own body is asking for, we unleash our inner advisor.

Our intention with these carefully honed activities is to bring your thoughts, emotions, inner sensations, wishes, and desires into harmony. Integrity, the felt experience of wholeness, arises from harmonious alignment. Creativity and co-creativity can then become the backdrop of your days. Play replaces power struggles, and discovery replaces repetitive patterns. You'll know you are on the right track with these activities if you notice feeling energized by your choices and enjoying more presence inside you and in your relationships.

Each process is simple to understand and easy to carry out; however, each of them has extraordinary power to inspire big relationship changes. Indeed, many professionals who graduate from our coaching programs tell us they use these activities as mainstays of their counseling work with couples and singles. Whether you use them personally or professionally, we simply urge you to *use* them. Any time you devote to the sincere study of your relationship life pays off hugely. We've tweaked the famous remark of the philosopher Tasso: any time spent on love is never wasted. We promise you that the time you spend to do these processes will not be wasted!

1. The Rule of Three Process: Getting New Insight into Your Relationships

When you want to make changes in your love life, it's helpful to know a good place to start. This activity is a good one for getting started because it not only shines a light on where your barriers are, it also takes you effortlessly on the first step to removing those barriers. The activity described in this section would fit neatly into one or two of your Ten-Minute Heart Talks, described in Chapter Eight.

The Rule of Three

Early in our careers as relationship counselors, we noticed that our clients often came in after failing repeatedly in trying to solve the same problem. For example, one couple told us that the problem that finally brought them in, chronic criticism, had actually repeated itself over and over since their first year of marriage. Now past 50 years of age, they estimated they had grappled with it hundreds of times without reducing the level of conflict in their relationship. For most people, though, it doesn't take hundreds of repetitions to wake them up to the urgency of solving a certain problem. We found that three instances carry about the same weight as a dozen. In other words, if you've experienced a pattern three or more times, it's time to wake up to the possibility that you've got an internally generated program that's running the show.

First, take a look at the basic concept beneath the process. The Rule of Three goes like this: if a pattern or problem has repeated three or more times in your love life (for example, if you've tried unsuccessfully dozens of times to get your husband to stop drinking, or you've been in several different relationships that ended the same way), consider it virtually certain that:

- The pattern or problem isn't about what you think it is, and in particular, it's got very little to do with the person you're playing it out with. An ancient, invisible, and unconscious program in *you* is directing the action as much as the other person is.

- *You* are doing specific actions that perpetuate the pattern.

- When *you* stop doing the actions that are perpetuating the problem, the problem will resolve itself, often by some previously unseen creative solution.

Here's an extreme example, which we'll follow with a more typical one. One of our seminar participants—we'll call her Anna—told us she got physically abused by her husband on numerous occasions until she put a stop to it once and for all with a specific action she took. We handed her the microphone, eager to find out how she had accomplished this miracle. However, when she came out with the eye-popping details, we were quick to jump in with a stern warning to the audience: "Don't try this at home."

After the occasion of her final beating, Anna went off to take a shower and returned to find her husband passed out drunk on the couch. She started to limp off to bed, but then she was seized by a creative notion. She soaked a sheet in cold water, put it on the floor and rolled him off the couch with a thud, getting barely a grunt out of him. She proceeded to roll him tightly in the wet sheet, like a mummy, so there was no possibility of movement when he came awake. Then she called every family member and friend she could find and invited them to come over.

It was a long night for all of them—probably most so for the man in the sheet—but at the end of it a reformed person emerged from his swaddled confines. He never touched her in anger again. According to Anna, the turning point for her husband came after hearing one person after another point to her bruised face and express disgust. They told him that should it ever happen again, he could expect no further communication from them.

That's an extreme situation, but the same kind of pattern goes on in more typical forms every day. For example, Patrick and Barb came in with a complaint about money arguments. As we explored with them, we found that they'd argued about money far more than three times—more like three times a week for the seven years of their relationship. They had met when they were both 45, and the money dramas began right away. Back then they had a convenient explanation for their money arguments. It was "because we didn't have any," said Patrick, with an agreeing head bob from Barb. "But then last week there was this moment when we were knee deep in one of our arguments and Barb said the damnedest thing," Patrick said, with a head shake of wonderment.

Barb said, "All of a sudden this thought struck me—here we are having the same money argument now as back when we didn't have any money to argue about. Now we're doing great, but we're still having the same argument."

We understood exactly what she meant, but we also knew something else: their hundreds of arguments about money didn't have much of anything to do with money. As we explored the issue with them at deeper levels, we encountered a typical destructive relationship paradigm at work: the struggle for control. In plain language, it's the need to have the other person say, in words or body language, "You're the boss." Some couples work this out temporarily by one party agreeing that the other one is boss. That solution usually doesn't work in the long term, because the non-boss partner eventually resents the one-up-one-down nature of the relationship. In Barb and Patrick's case, though, both of them had the same driving need to be boss, a perfect setup for long-running conflict.

They could just as easily have picked sex or chores as the focal point of their struggles for boss-hood, but money struggles became their main battleground. However, once we showed them how their money fights were really about control, they saw that the real problem, in Barb's poetic words, was their "eternal, infernal struggle to be right." They told us that bickering about who was right and who was wrong extended back to their very first date, when they had an argument about the amount to tip the waiter.

Once they realized their money fights didn't really have anything to do with money, they lost their fascination with arguing about it.

The patterns that repeat themselves over and over in your relationships are a gold mine of information for you. This activity gives you an outline so you can get the maximum amount of treasured learning out of the experience.

Instructions

Get your favorite writing materials and sit down, either with a partner or by yourself. We often recommend doing the process by yourself, even if you have a partner you do it with some of the time too. Sometimes it takes solitude to get to the depths of yourself that this process can reveal to you. On the other hand, we've seen some of the biggest breakthroughs happen between couples who have never before actually sat down and carried out any kind of transformational activity.

When you're ready, begin asking the following series of questions. If you're doing this with a partner, take turns asking the questions out loud. If you're doing the process by yourself, we also recommend saying the questions aloud.

Question 1: *What have I complained about in our relationship (or if single, in my relationships in the past) three or more times?*

After you ask the question aloud, focus your awareness back on yourself. Scan your present and past for things you've complained about three or more times: chores not getting done, showing up late, not doing what h/she said they'd do, and the like.

Write down on paper the complaints you come up with. A simple descriptor will do:

- Drinking too much at parties
- Not doing fair share of housework
- Not participating in kids' activities

Once you've got your list, move on to the next question.

Question 2: *What have I complained about in our relationship (or if single, in my relationships in the past) three or more times that still has not changed?*

This question helps you look for the crystallized patterns, the ones that have not changed in spite of many complaints on your part. Many people discover in this process that almost all of their biggest, most recycling complaints are about things that are still continuing to bother them.

Make a list of your complaints that have not resulted in positive behavior change on anyone's part, which may be the pared-down version of your list from Question 1. If you have more than one item, pick the biggest one to work on first. For example, if your mate's drinking has been resistant to three or more complaints on your part, you would pick that one ahead of complaints such as not remembering to walk the dog.

Get your biggest complaint-that-hasn't-changed clearly in your mind and proceed to the next question.

Question 3: *In what ways am I supporting and enabling my partner in continuing to do the thing I'm complaining about?*

(If single, ask it this way: In what ways have I in the past supported and enabled relationship partners in doing the things I was complaining about?)

You will likely discover—as we did, and thousands of our seminar participants have—that you have some old limiting belief stashed away in your unconscious that's requiring you to repeat a negative pattern. For example, Gay grew up around family members who practiced alcohol and tobacco addictions: "I was a heavy smoker even before I was born. Mom was seldom seen without a cigarette in hand, and when I was a teenager I started bumming smokes from her bounteous supply of unfiltered Camels. In my early twenties I did a one-eighty and became a militant nonsmoker, but some unconscious belief was still lurking in the depths of my consciousness, one that said: You must always be in a close relationship with an addict."

How did he figure that out? "Because I got into more than three relationships in which I didn't have an addiction but my partner did! In one relationship I managed to remain oblivious to my partner smoking cigarettes and abusing Valium for most of a year. I just thought her breath was always super minty and that she would occasionally be in a super-mellow mood. Finally when I woke up out of the pattern, I realized that I had an unconscious requirement to be close to an addict, based on my early conditioning. That insight gave me the freedom to create the first addiction-free relationship in my life, one that's still going strong thirty-plus years later!"

The bottom line: ancient forces within us cause us to participate unconsciously in maintaining the very issues we are complaining about. When we first had this insight, it didn't fill us with joy right away. At first we found it so uncomfortable to acknowledge that we were co-conspirators in keeping alive the very things we were complaining about. But face it we did, as most of us ultimately will if we expect to mature in our ability to love and be loved.

Question 4: *If I weren't using my energy to complain about this issue, what creative purpose could I put that energy toward?*

This question gives you a glimpse of the future. Ultimately the question is whether you can withdraw attention from complaining and redirect that energy into creative activities. If you think of rechanneling the energy into something more creative, you avoid the trap of making yourself wrong for things you've done in the past. You've simply been using your energy inefficiently, expending effort to control things you have no control over. When you withdraw energy from trying to control the uncontrollable, you free up massive attention you can put into more positive things.

Question 5: *What simple action step can I take in the next day to start moving toward my creative purpose?*

This question puts your learning into action in your relationships right now. This is where the rubber meets the road and your inner changes become visible in your daily choices. Taking a measurable step toward what you really want has great power to change your life, so start now and then celebrate your step.

2. The Love Catalyst for Couples: A Deep Experience of Full-Spectrum Presencing

Although this activity is primarily a deep experience of being present, our students began calling it the Love Catalyst, for reasons that may become clearer after you practice it. What they noticed was that a deep experience of being present often came with a powerful side effect: they felt a deeper flow of love in the depths of themselves and between them and their partners. We hope you'll take the time to savor the riches of the activity.

This practice can be done repeatedly over time. You can practice solo or with a mate, friend, or colleague. This is primarily an expansive practice rather than a corrective one to handle problems, though it does open up much quicker problem solving. As you deepen your practice, you may notice an expanded experience of awareness.

For example, people have reported that being able to feel their Full-Spectrum Presence makes it easier to resonate with a completely different point of view or feeling state in another. People have been delighted to report that they don't get thrown off by the actions or emotions of others they are close to, and that they experience a deeper sense of rapport and empathy. They have noticed easy access to new solutions and creative possibilities with partners, and they've found they have renewal resources on tap as their practice begins to create new habits.

Instructions

Start by becoming aware of the physical aspects of your body. Tune in to your muscles and bones, give attention to the surface of your skin, become aware of the places where your body touches the chair or whatever you're resting on.

Now rest your awareness beneath the surface and feel the energy of your body, all its feelings and sensations. Trillions of interactions are happening inside you right now. Tune in to the feeling of all those interactions and all the tiny vibrations they give off.

Now rest your awareness on the energy of your breathing. Feel the movements of your breath. You might feel your breathing in your chest, or the rising and falling of your belly, or the feeling of the air in your nostrils as it goes in and out. Rest your awareness on the easy flow of your breathing, in and out.

Now rest your awareness on the feeling of your in-breath and the feeling of your out-breath. Let yourself notice also the rollover points where the in-breath melts into the out-breath, and where the out-breath melts into the in-breath. If you notice any pauses, smooth those out so there's no gap in the rollover from out to in and in to out.

Now notice the duration of your in-breath, and the duration of your out-breath. For the next few moments see if you can find a balance, so that the in-breath and the out-breath are about the same length. Let your in-breath melt into the out-breath with no gap or pause, and let your out-breath melt into your in-breath.

As you breathe, let your breath welcome all the sensations and feelings inside your body. Notice the sensations you feel in your back and shoulders. Notice whether your awareness of what you feel carries any judgment or criticism. If possible, free yourself from judgment and just tune in generously to whatever you're feeling.

Let your awareness move as easily as opening and closing your eyes. Eyes closed, notice your breathing. Eyes open, notice something in the room. Eyes closed, notice a body sensation. Eyes open, notice something else in the room. Repeat this for a minute or so . . .

Now keep your eyes open and let them be softly relaxed as if they were floating in your head. Take several easy breaths, noticing where your breath travels in your body. Easily shift your attention to something in the room, letting your attention rest on that. Then shift your attention back to your breathing, all with your eyes softly open.

Place your sensitive awareness on you with your in-breath. Then let your attention shift to someone or something outside you on the out-breath. Repeat a few times . . .

Now let your breathing flow easily as you shift your generous attention to your partner. Give your full awareness to every aspect of your partner's being. Be aware of the physicality of your partner. Simply give your generous attention to the physical aspects of your partner, becoming aware of him or her as a physical being.

Now shift your attention back to yourself. Give your generous attention to the physical aspects of yourself. Become really aware of yourself as a physical being.

And now shift your attention back to your partner. Be aware of your partner as an energy being. Beneath the surface are all the emotions and sensations your partner feels and we all feel. There are dozens of other currents and hums and vibrations of trillions of interactions happening inside your partner. Tune in to your partner as a being filled with energy and emotion and sensation.

Move your awareness around you and then around your partner in an infinity sign. Imagine the infinity figure eight swirling easily around like a languid river that first touches you, then touches your partner.

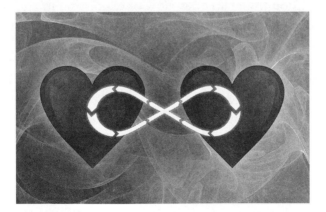

Imagine the infinity sign resting at your pelvis area. As you give your curious awareness to you, notice your body sensations and feelings all through your pelvis. Genuinely wonder about how you can enjoy your full sexual and creative flow.

Then allow your appreciative attention to flow around your partner, presencing his or her pelvis. As you let your curious attention move toward and around your partner, appreciate his or her sexual and creative juiciness flourishing.

Shift your flowing, curious awareness to loop toward and around your partner's belly, then loop the infinity swirl of awareness around your belly, then back to your partner in a continuous, easy loop of attention. Let yourself presence what's new, what's emerging, welcoming the flutters of fear and excitement in the belly.

Then shift your flowing, curious awareness to loop toward and around your partner's heart area, then loop the infinity swirl of awareness around your heart and shoulder blade area, then back to your partner in a continuous, easy loop of attention. As you give your generous awareness to you and to your partner, let yourself open the gates of gratitude, giving and receiving love freely and fully.

Now shift your flowing, curious awareness to loop toward and around your partner's throat and back of the neck, then loop the infinity swirl of awareness around your throat area, then back to your partner in a continuous, easy loop of attention. Let your generous attention invite an open flow of expressing in and between you. Welcome authentic flow and celebrate realness as you loop your awareness.

Then shift your flowing, curious awareness to loop toward and around your partner's eyes and back of the head, then loop the infinity swirl of awareness around your eye area, then back to your partner in a continuous, easy loop of attention. As you loop, open a flow of appreciating essence. Appreciate who you are at your core and who your partner is at his or her core as you let your awareness easily flow around both of you.

Shift your flowing, curious awareness to loop toward and around the top of your partner's head, then loop the infinity swirl of awareness around the area just above and around your head, then back to your partner in a continuous, easy loop of attention. As you gently loop your awareness, open an intention to celebrate your highest evolution and your partner's creative fulfillment.

Now become aware of the flow of connection between you, feeling how all the energy and vibrations of your being are connecting and interacting with all the energy and vibrations of your partner. Tune in to those flowing, streaming waves of connection between you. Feel how they flow, connect, dance, and harmonize together.

As you feel the energy inside you and your partner, notice also that there's a vast open space inside you. It's the stillness of pure consciousness, behind and within and around all the trillions of interactions and vibrations. All your energy and vibrations are happening in a big open space. You can actually feel that vast open space as you tune in and listen innocently for it.

As you feel the vast open space inside you, your partner is also feeling that vast open space. Be aware of your vast open inner space and the vast open inner space of your partner at the same time.

Now include the space between you in your awareness, and the space around you. Rest for a few moments, sharing space with your partner.

3. The Love Catalyst for Singles: Full-Spectrum Presencing to Attract the Love of Your Life

If you're single, investing 20 minutes in this experiential process could be the step you need to open up a new world of intimacy for you. The activity brings the full power of your consciousness to bear upon attracting the ideal mate into your life.

Instructions

Take a moment now to get comfortable and open your mind to new learning. Take a few easy breaths and let them settle down inside you so you can give your full attention to the process.

The purpose of this activity is to assist you in drawing a healthy loving relationship into your life, effortlessly, without stressful pursuit, by making three inner shifts that create powerful results in your life.

Begin with a few moments of getting centered, relaxed, and open to discovery and exploration. Begin to be aware now of the physical aspects of your body. Be aware of the meat of your muscles, the surface of your skin, and all the places where your body touches the chair or whatever you're resting on.

Rest your awareness beneath the surface of your skin and feel the energy of your body, all its feelings and sensations. Trillions of interactions are happening inside you right now. Tune in to the feeling of all those interactions and the millions of tiny vibrations they're giving off.

Rest your awareness now on your breathing. Feel the movement of your breath. You might feel it in your chest or your belly or around your nostrils as it goes in and out. Rest your awareness on the easy flow of your breathing, in and out.

Now rest your awareness on the feeling of your in-breath and the feeling of your out-breath. Notice also the rollover point where the in-breath melts into the out-breath, and where the out-breath melts into the in-breath.

Now notice the duration of the in-breath and the duration of the out-breath. For the next few moments, see if you can find a balance, so that the in-breath and out-breath are about the same length. Let the in-breath roll right over into the out-breath with no gap or pause.

Let your awareness move as easily as opening and closing your eyes. Eyes closed, notice your breathing. Eyes open, notice something in the room. Eyes closed, notice a body sensation. Eyes open, notice something else in the room. Repeat this for a minute or so . . .

Now keep your eyes open and let them be soft in your head. Take several easy breaths, noticing where your breath travels in your body. Easily shift your attention to something in the room, letting your attention rest on that. Then shift your attention back to your breathing, all with your eyes softly open.

Place your sensitive awareness on you with your in-breath. Then let your attention shift to someone or something outside you on the out-breath. Repeat a few times . . .

Here's the first inner shift: as you relax into your breathing, open your mind to a new experience of commitment. To successfully make a powerful change in your life, begin with sincerely committing to that change. Consciously committing to attract genuine love into your life greatly enhances your chances of turning your dream into reality.

For the next few minutes, you'll form a specific commitment in your mind, then give your curious attention to the feelings and sensations in your body. Here's the specific commitment we'd like you to embrace:

I commit to feeling genuine love in my life all the time.

Say it to yourself again:

I commit to feeling genuine love in my life all the time.

You may want to phrase it differently later, or to shape the words and concepts to your own taste. For now, though, let's use this one:

I commit to feeling genuine love in my life all the time.

Now here's how to do it: say the sentence in your mind quietly in your own voice, then pause for 10 or 15 seconds and feel how your body responds to the commitment. By doing this you can discover whether your body and mind are in agreement about your willingness to feel genuine love all the time.

There are no right or wrong ways for your body to respond. Just let your body's sensations and feelings arise, and then repeat the sentence again in your mind. So, again, say the following sentence quietly in your mind: I commit to feeling genuine love in my life all the time.

Now let go of the words in your mind and shift your attention to your body. Rest your sensitive awareness on your body sensations and feelings, just listening to and appreciating your body. Repeat this sequence another few times.

And now let's continue to inner shift number two. Once you feel genuinely committed, the next thing to do is remove the major barrier to enjoying genuine love in your life. The major barrier to a loving relationship with another person is any unloved part of yourself. An aspect of ourselves that we've never loved and accepted keeps us from forming and keeping genuine love from others.

Here's why: if you don't love yourself, you'll always be looking for someone else to do it for you. It never works, though, because people who don't love themselves attract people who don't love themselves. Then they try to get the other person to love them unconditionally, when they're not even doing it for themselves.

When you love yourself deeply and unconditionally, for everything you are and everything you aren't, you attract people into your life who love and accept themselves. If you feel fundamentally unlovable deep down inside, you'll attract a lover who feels the same way.

When we don't love some part of ourselves, we run around in desperation trying to get someone else to love us. Our hope is that if they give us enough love, our unlovable part will go away. It never does. Only a moment of loving ourselves unconditionally will do that particular job.

Fortunately, you can solve that problem right here and right now. What are you feeling right now? Tune in to yourself and do a quick body scan. Are you afraid that this practice may not work for you? Are you afraid that nothing will work? Are you worried that maybe you're not good enough to have genuine love in your life?

Do you fear, as we once did, that there's something fundamentally wrong with you that's always going to keep you from love?

Right now, feel all those feelings, or whatever else you feel, and love your feelings exactly as they are. Love yourself for having them. Love yourself for having the courage to feel.

We've never met anyone who loved him- or herself deeply and unconditionally all the time. Don't expect that you'll be perfect at it either. Begin with a second or two of loving yourself and work up from there. Think of someone you know you love, and give yourself that same embrace of love. With practice, your own ability to love and accept yourself will grow and grow. All it takes is one little drop of love, and your life begins to change.

So now we'll proceed to inner shift number three. To create a lasting love relationship, you need to get clear on what qualities you would like in your mate. You also need to get clear on what qualities you do not want in a mate.

We'll begin with your three absolute yeses. What are three things you most want in a mate, the things on the top of your list? Those are your three absolute yeses. Right now, just think about them for a moment. You could write them down later, or make them up now.

Ask yourself: *What's my first absolute yes? What's the absolutely most important thing I want in a mate?* Then ask yourself: *What's my second absolute yes? What's the second most important thing that I want in a mate?* And finally, ask yourself: *What's the third most important thing that I really want in a mate?*

Now, take a moment and honestly look and see whether you enjoy in yourself the qualities you most want in your mate. For example, if one of your three absolute yeses is honesty, check inside and make sure you practice being impeccably honest. If beauty is important to you, find out if you feel beautiful, from your surface to your soul. Be frank with yourself. If you find yourself coming up short on some of the qualities you're seeking in a mate, you're setting yourself up for disappointment. Remember, like attracts like, so focus on becoming inside like the person you want to attract from the outside.

And now take a moment to form your three absolute nos. These are just as important as your yeses. If you're clear about what you don't want in your life, you'll avoid repeating the same mistakes over and over.

What are three things you absolutely do not want to invite into your life? What are three things you will wake up celebrating the absence of in your life? So consider: *The most important thing I vow never to invite into my life again is*_____. And then wonder. *The second most important thing I vow never to invite into my life is* _____. *And the third most important thing I vow never to invite into my life is* _____. You can think about these things now, or write them down later, after you've completed this practice. Whatever you do, though, be frank with yourself.

Are you clear on your three absolute nos? If not, do some more reflecting on what's essential for you to keep out of your love life. Ultimately, you need to forgive yourself and accept what you've created in the past. Obsessing about the past consumes your precious energy. You need to reclaim all that energy to have a full tank for your new relationship journey, for fueling the benign creative outburst your life can become. You may refine your absolute yeses and nos as you explore, and for now, celebrate your creation of this powerful foundation for choosing conscious love.

4. The Genius of Relationship Process: Liberating Your Hidden Creativity

After midlife the issue of discovering your own unique, creative contribution—what we call your "genius"—becomes crucial to your individual well-being and the health of your relationships. At midlife we begin to grow more aware of our own mortality, and along with that awareness comes an increased pressure from within to develop ourselves to our highest potential. Of course, many people take a look at that challenge and give up, sliding into the kind of stagnation and despair that Erik Erikson says is the result of ignoring our inner creative urges in our 50s and 60s.

The Genius of Relationship Process is a direct antidote to any kind of stagnation and despair. It opens up two territories that most people have never explored: your individual creative genius and the genius of your relationships. In other words, most people have never paused to identify consciously what the full flowering of their own creative lives and their relationship lives would look like. The process explores inner territory that becomes especially important to map out at midlife and beyond. Up until the mid-40s it is usually possible to build a successful life by learning how to play roles well—student, employee, entrepreneur, parent. At midlife and beyond, though, the rewards come more from getting free of the strictures of roles than from learning how to play them better.

Couples who invest 20 minutes in doing the Genius of Relationship Process tell us it opens the gateway to a new dimension of creativity and positive feeling in their relationship. Singles who do the Genius of Relationship Process report that the exercise snaps into focus, often for the first time, the quality of relationship they most want to manifest.

Unlocking Genius with the Creative Toss

This process is based on a new paradigm: relationships are about nurturing the creative flow within and between the people involved. The old paradigm of relationship relies on control and power moves, both of which ultimately limit the possibilities of intimacy. The players vie for adrenaline spikes by controlling, being right, and using other territorial strategies. Most power players will ultimately call off connection by threatening or making an abrupt departure.

The Creative Toss allows you, whether you are single or in a relationship, to generate new moves and keep the relationship game going. Tossing generates more choices, interrupts old habits, feeds your fun fountain, and creates confidence that you can continue expanding and enjoying discoveries in relating.

Tossing can become the primary activity of your relationship. Tossing allows you to give and receive love, play, discovery—all the sparks that make day-to-day relationships deepen in value.

Think of each interaction as an opportunity to give and receive a toss. You can either stop the game or keep it going, by tossing in a way that makes it difficult for the receiver or in a way that notices the timing and delivery that will make receiving easy and even pleasurable. As the receiver of the toss, you can stop the collaboration by getting distracted, letting the toss bounce off, or not being ready in other ways: not being response-able to receive. Or you can give your attention to the toss and do whatever you can to fully receive. When people do tossing well, they create magic, and even when they're just starting and feel awkward, they generate more fun, play, and possibility.

Getting Primed

Get a few party balloons and blow them up. Once they're fully inflated, take a few minutes to toss a balloon back and forth to each other. Put a priority on having fun tossing the balloon back and forth. Discover how long you can go before something happens to stop the flow of fun.

When this occurs, take note of how it happened. Everyone has favorite ways of stopping the flow—just notice what your way was of stopping the game of toss.

Here are a few ways the flow gets stopped:

- Not looking at the balloon or your partner for signals

- Keeping the balloon and neglecting to actually toss it

- Tossing the balloon in a completely different direction from where your partner is standing

- Distracting yourself (texting, answering the phone or e-mail, going into the other room)

- Criticizing the way your partner is tossing

After you've taken note of how you stopped the flow, take a few breaths and regroup. Once you feel centered again, try on a new set of intentions: what can I do to keep the tossing game going with my partner while we invent new and creative tosses to each other?

Actively try on these intentions as you toss the balloon back and forth. Notice the upsurge in energy and connection you feel when you keep the toss going in creative new directions for a while.

Adding Words

We recommend adding words *after* you spend some time playing nonverbally so you get an embodied sense of what you are creating together, a shared wholeness and commitment to connect.

If you'd like to go further with this activity, here's how to take it into verbal communication.

First, select a speaker and a receiver.

Speaker, you'll talk about something you want to create in your relationship, something you want to share or discuss. After doing this activity dozens of times with hundreds of people, we highly recommend this sequence:

Speaker, share one out-breath of words and toss the balloon when you've completed your sentence or phrase.

Receiver, select one of the following sentences and toss these words *only* with the balloon back to the speaker:

- "Tell me more."

- "What interested you most about that?"

- "Then what happened (or happens)?"

Receiver, do your best to add curiosity to your toss and to the words, and to *avoid* adding other phrases such as "What were you thinking?" or "Why would you want to do that?!" Just the three phrases above are amazingly effective at keeping the game going, and you can repeat and mix and match them.

We recommend that you start with one to two minutes for tossing with words, then shift roles.

What can you expect from a longer-term practice of tossing? In improvisational theater, actors practice a game that is based on "Yes, and . . ." It's a form of tossing. Whatever one actor says to his or her partner, the partner receives with a whole-body yes. *Yes, this is what's true now. Yes, this suggestion is my world in this moment.* The receiver takes in the statement and then adds to it. That's the "and." New worlds open, and new perspectives get added to your world. Instead of arguing with what's happening, a favorite relationship sport, tossing allows you to fully receive your partner's world right now, and to add to that. In an online article about the German soccer team's success, the author, Otto Scharmer, an advocate of the power of presencing in business, wrote a description that sounds like the results of advanced tossing:

> So what is driving the success of the German team? It's a philosophy that requires all players to operate from a *shared awareness of the evolving whole.* Everyone is required to be aware of what's happening everywhere on the field—the changing positions, the emerging spaces among their own team members and their opponents, to keep the ball moving. It's that shared awareness of the evolving whole that allows them to pass the ball faster than the opposing team at times can comprehend, or react to. It was the chief reason the Brazil defense collapsed and conceded four goals in six minutes of the semifinal this week.

The German team went on to win the World Cup and create some amazing images of brilliant tossing for the world to enjoy. They proved you can create more synergy and collaboration in your own world with tossing.

Why not give it a toss and see what kind of miracles you can perform in the World Cup of your life?

5. Unhooking the Source: That Was Then, This Is Now

At midlife and beyond, awareness of change becomes more acute. Friends die, careers change and end, and every day brings shifts and completions that can accumulate like old files in the garage of your consciousness.

This simple yet profound activity supports you in getting current with your life and releasing the past, unhooking the triggers and memories from old painful events in a friendly way so you can be present to the opportunities to savor giving and receiving love today.

Instructions

Each time you go through this activity, start by identifying something you are willing to release and place firmly in the past. It could be a person, an event, a memory that troubles you, or an interaction that you keep picking over. When you ruminate on them or try to change the past, all these things decrease the vitality and joy you experience. When you let go and get present, you'll notice you expand your capacity for intimacy and juiciness in the now.

This activity is best done standing.

First, ask your body which direction is the past. Use one hand and turn to point toward the past and that event, saying,

"That was then."

Then turn or step to stand in the present and use your other hand to touch your chest and say,

"This is now."

Again, point toward the past and say, "That was then," and turn to stand in the present, using your other hand to touch your chest as you say, "This is now."

Continue this sequence as you use your voice and gestures to emphasize different words. Use your whole body to participate and vary the rhythm and speed of the words. Explore different styles of turning and moving as you put the past in the past and stand in now. Dare we say it?—have fun with the activity!

You'll know from your body signals when you've completed it. You'll feel a shift in your body that you can notice, such as a big, easy breath, a feeling of warmth and space, or an inner smile. Continue playing with "That was then" and "This is now" until *you* feel the shift. Everyone's change sequence is different, and as you explore you'll find more body intelligence expanding and informing you in this activity and generally in your life.

Sometimes you'll take on a biggie, something that happened that had a big impact on you or wounded you deeply. Those events may require several rounds of That Was Then as you uncover different layers and aspects of the issue. We've found that even the most brambly problem yields to the playful repetition of this sequence if you let your whole body explore.

Variations

Sometimes you want to let go of a person or people. Your sequence would then look like this:

First, ask your body which direction is the past. Use one hand and point toward the past and that event, saying,

"That was them." Or *"That was him/her."*

Then stand in the present and use your other hand to touch your chest and say,

"This is me."

Again, point toward the past and say, "That was them," and turn to stand in the present, using your other hand to touch your chest as you say, "This is me."

Another variation that our seminar participants have enjoyed handles the pesky issue of getting in each other's business, or, as one of our clients put it, "getting up in his grille." So in this case you'd follow this sequence to let go of things over which you have little to no control, which frees you to choose actions that have the greatest effectiveness.

First, ask your body which direction is the past. Use one hand and point toward the past and that event, saying,

"That's his business." Or *"That's her business."*

Then stand in the present and use your other hand to touch your chest as you say,

"This is my business."

Again, point toward the past and say, "That's his/her business," and turn to stand in the present, using your other hand to touch your chest as you say, "This is my business."

As you practice That Was Then, you might find that waves of emotion or mental flashes of memory dart through your mind. These experiences are common and a natural result of releasing old patterns and opening your body intelligence for new experiences and connections. We suggest breathing and riding the waves as they move through. You don't need to do anything except presence them and let them float by.

6. Customizing Your Appreciation: The Most Reliable Way to Renew Intimacy

Appreciation can replace control and conflict and give you way more bang for the buck in your close relationships. It answers the question, "What are you going to do with the free time you've generated by ending blame and criticism?" People blossom when they are appreciated. We know that, and most of us do our best to appreciate those close to us, whether they are mates, family, friends, or colleagues. What if you had a way to fit your appreciation like a soft glove to the other's hand or make a gesture that elicits the "How did you know?!" smile of gratitude? This activity—a short but revealing interview you conduct with another person—deepens your understanding of your friend, date, or partner so that your appreciation creates the most positive impact and generates ever more flow of connection between you. We've used it in many seminars over the years and find that people immediately see more appreciation possibilities. Many use this interview repeatedly over time as a way to continue discovering new things to appreciate.

We suggest that you schedule a convenient time for your interview(s), and that you check in periodically to see if any of the parameters have changed or evolved as you deepen your appreciation practice. Each interview will take approximately 15 minutes, and you may want to do just one at a time to really savor the experience. Most people like the interviewer to record their answers in either written or audio formats that can be revisited for appreciation inspiration.

1. How do you most like to be appreciated:

    a. Verbally, written, or . . . ?

    b. Alone, with your partner, with friends, in public or . . . ?

    c. With or without props (flowers, cards, orchestra)?

2. What body sensations let you know you are expanding your capacity to receive appreciation?

3. What does your partner do/say that really works to appreciate you?

4. What timing do you like best for appreciations? For example, do you like to receive appreciations regularly, be surprised by them, or get a bunch at once?

5. Which of your qualities, skills, and attributes would you like to be appreciated more?

6. What seemingly "wrong" qualities about you, things you've tried to change or get rid of, would you be open to having appreciated? For example, you might judge something about your body or tone of voice, or the way you do certain activities.

7. What's the current frequency of appreciation in your relationship? Would you like to place a different order? Okay, go ahead and place the new order or affirm the current frequency.

8. On a daily basis, what actions/events produce the highest level of feeling appreciated for you? (Hint to interviewer: focus on those when you are appreciating the person you're interviewing.)

Appendix B

The Four Pillars of Integrity

When we started working and teaching together in 1980, we were intently interested in creating new communication and operational structures that demonstrably enhanced the experience of wholeness, the root meaning of integrity. We came to see that integrity is made up of measurable skills that can be learned and can be implemented to recover wholeness when problems arise.

These skills have been tested and refined for over 30 years with hundreds of students, couples, partners, business leaders, entrepreneurs, and people wanting to live lives in alignment with essence and in harmony with others and the world. We offer these as questions that can generate discovery and easy application. Our students and clients have found that focusing on one skill at a time gives them a chance to see the difference that integrity makes and to build their experience of wholeness in easy chunks.

Emotional Literacy

This pillar creates a structure of transparency in your own experience and interactions with others.

- How can I notice what I'm actually feeling and experiencing in the moment?

- How can I reliably discern between different emotions and sensations (e.g., between hunger and fear)?

- How can I learn to locate emotions accurately in my body (e.g., "anger" in neck/shoulders, "sadness" in chest/throat, "fear" in belly)?

- In what ways can I give myself attention when a feeling is emerging, and let my emotions show?

- How can I follow my sensations/emotions to their source using my attention and body wisdom (even when it seems obvious that the source is the other person)?

- How can I speak about my feelings and inner experience congruently so that others comprehend?

- To what extent can I consistently practice being with feelings until they flow through to completion (instead of drowning them out with food, TV, tweets, or other distractions)?

Healthy Response-ability

The skills in this pillar move you from reactivity and recycling blame and criticism to the genuine ability to respond fully to your life and relationships.

- How can I respond freely with full presence rather than react automatically?

- How many ways can I shift from defensiveness to openness to learning?

- How can I shift readily and easily from blame to wonder?

- How can my being inspire others to take 100 percent response-ability?

Impeccable Agreements

Making and keeping effective agreements can add immeasurably to clarity and ease in your daily life.

- Hmmm, how can I experience the connection between keeping my agreements and increased aliveness (rather than thinking of agreements as rules other people are making me follow)?
- How do I make a conscious agreement?
- How can I easily say no to agreements I don't want to make?
- In what ways can I reference my whole-body wisdom to select agreements I do want to make?
- How can I consciously change agreements that are not working?

Speaking from Discovery and Listening Appreciatively

If you'd like to speak in a way that your partner and others will receive, and listen in a way that invites others to share deeply with you, these skills will build a deeper level of communication.

- How can I learn to communicate in a way that closely matches my actual experience?
- How can I learn to speak about the details of what is going on in any given moment in a way that invites wonder and is free of blame?
- In what manner can I give active awareness to how my communications are landing?
- How can I source and initiate authentic speaking in any situation (e.g., speaking from discovery without being begged, threatened, or coerced)?

- How can I sense and use the body sensations and experiences associated with authenticity as guides, and those associated with withholding as signals to shift?

- In what ways can I speak from discovery and listen appreciatively, even under duress?

- How can I listen accurately, appreciatively, and in a way that invites wonder?

- Am I willing to choose revealing over concealing?

Further Resources

Our websites and Facebook pages offer many additional resources for deepening your experiential understanding of integrity and harmony. For example, we have created videos for the integrity skills we've explored here and short videos that explore how to listen, how to tell the truth, and how *not* to do both, as well as other common relationship issues. Our Facebook pages contain daily relationship tips and a place to share your experiences and enjoy support for your deepening experience of creative fulfillment. Enjoy.

www.hendricks.com

www.foundationforconsciousliving.com

On Facebook: Hearts in Harmony with Katie and Gay Hendricks
www.facebook.com/fclconnect

Acknowledgments

First, a deep bow of gratitude to the many people who have read our relationship books, attended our seminars, and practiced the principles and processes we teach. Thank you for showing how love can keep deepening and expanding throughout the human lifespan.

We also wish to thank the colleagues and three generations of students we've had the pleasure of working with over the past 45 years. Your input, examples, stories, and questions added immeasurable richness to our work.

Gratitude as always to Bonnie Solow, agent of our dreams and dear friend of the family.

We love the team at Hay House! Thanks in particular to Reid Tracy for many years of friendship and good advice, to Patty Gift for her heart and vision, and to Anne Barthel for her impeccable touch on the page and making the editing process fun.

About the Authors

Gay Hendricks, Ph.D., and **Kathlyn Hendricks, Ph.D.**, are pioneers in the fields of conscious relationships and body intelligence and the authors of more than 30 books, including bestsellers such as *Conscious Loving, The Big Leap*, and *Five Wishes*. During the past 30 years they have appeared on hundreds of radio and television shows and networks, including *Oprah*, CNN, CNBC, and CBS's *48 Hours*. In 1989 they founded The Hendricks Institute, which offers seminars annually in North America, Asia, and Europe. Their nonprofit organization, the Foundation for Conscious Living, funds research, films, and scholarships in the areas of conscious relationships and natural well-being. The Hendrickses live in Ojai, California. Learn more at www.hendricks.com.

Hay House Titles of Related Interest

YOU CAN HEAL YOUR LIFE, the movie, starring Louise Hay & Friends
(available as a 1-DVD program and an expanded 2-DVD set)
Watch the trailer at: www.LouiseHayMovie.com

THE SHIFT, the movie,
starring Dr. Wayne W. Dyer
(available as a 1-DVD program and an expanded 2-DVD set)
Watch the trailer at: www.DyerMovie.com

*A FIELD GUIDE TO HAPPINESS: What I Learned in Bhutan about
Living, Loving, and Waking Up,* by Linda Leaming

*GODDESSES NEVER AGE: The Secret Prescription for Radiance,
Vitality, and Well-Being,* by Christiane Northrup, M.D.

*REWIRE YOUR BRAIN FOR LOVE: Creating Vibrant Relationships
Using the Science of Mindfulness,* by Marsha Lucas, Ph.D.

*TALK Rx: Five Steps to Honest Conversations That Create Connection,
Health, and Happiness,* by Neha Sangwan, M.D.

All of the above are available at your local bookstore,
or may be ordered by contacting Hay House (see next page).

We hope you enjoyed this Hay House book.
If you'd like to receive our online catalog featuring
additional information on Hay House books and products,
or if you'd like to find out more about the
Hay Foundation, please contact:

Hay House, Inc., P.O. Box 5100, Carlsbad, CA 92018-5100
(760) 431-7695 or (800) 654-5126
(760) 431-6948 (fax) or (800) 650-5115 (fax)
www.hayhouse.com® • www.hayfoundation.org

Published and distributed in Australia by: Hay House Australia Pty. Ltd.,
18/36 Ralph St., Alexandria NSW 2015
Phone: 612-9669-4299 • *Fax:* 612-9669-4144 • www.hayhouse.com.au

Published and distributed in the United Kingdom by: Hay House UK, Ltd.,
Astley House, 33 Notting Hill Gate, London W11 3JQ
Phone: 44-20-3675-2450 • *Fax:* 44-20-3675-2451 • www.hayhouse.co.uk

Published and distributed in the Republic of South Africa by: Hay House SA
(Pty), Ltd., P.O. Box 990, Witkoppen 2068
info@hayhouse.co.za • www.hayhouse.co.za

Published in India by: Hay House Publishers India,
Muskaan Complex, Plot No. 3, B-2, Vasant Kunj, New Delhi 110 070
Phone: 91-11-4176-1620 • *Fax:* 91-11-4176-1630 • www.hayhouse.co.in

Distributed in Canada by: Raincoast Books,
2440 Viking Way, Richmond, B.C. V6V 1N2
Phone: 1-800-663-5714 • *Fax:* 1-800-565-3770 • www.raincoast.com

Take Your Soul on a Vacation

Visit www.HealYourLife.com® to regroup, recharge,
and reconnect with your own magnificence.
Featuring blogs, mind-body-spirit news, and
life-changing wisdom from Louise Hay and friends.

Visit www.HealYourLife.com today!